32

BOOKS BY HENRY SLOANE COFFIN

WHAT CRUCIFIED CHRIST?

THE MEANING OF THE CROSS

BY

HENRY SLOANE COFFIN

BROWN PROFESSOR OF HOMILETICS AND PRESIDENT OF THE
FACULTY OF THE UNION THEOLOGICAL SEMINARY,
NEW YORK, N. Y.

NEW YORK
CHARLES SCRIBNER'S SONS
1931

TO
MY COLLEAGUES
IN THE FACULTY OF UNION THEOLOGICAL SEMINARY

ADIUTORIBUS QUI MIHI SOLATIO SUNT

FOREWORD

THE substance of the following chapters has been given in various forms to companies of ministers and theological students and to other groups of thoughtful Christians in a dozen or more centres in the United States and Canada. The only excuse for rewriting and publishing has been the request of a number of listeners, representing different communions and widely differing points of view, that they might have the material in permanent form to study and think over and adapt for their own uses. No one is more aware than I of the inadequacy of the volume as a comprehensive treatment of the meaning of the chief event in the historic Gospel: *et ad haec quis tam idoneus?* My hope is that my attempt to put the meaning of the cross in terms intelligible and moving to the men of to-day will start others to make similar but more enlightening and affecting interpretations.

HENRY SLOANE COFFIN.

NEW YORK,
January, 1931.

CONTENTS

CONTENTS

THE MEANING OF THE CROSS

CHAPTER I

SOME years ago a well-known British journalist, the late W. T. Stead, after witnessing the Passion Play at Oberammergau, came away saying to himself: "This is the story which has transformed the world." And he seemed to hear an echo from the Bavarian hills about him: "Yes, and will transform it."

Each generation stresses particular aspects of the Gospel; and it must be confessed that in our day, and especially in those circles where Christianity is interpreted in terms of contemporary thought, the cross does not hold the central place in preaching. With many men the Incarnation has taken the place formerly occupied by the Atonement, and the character of Jesus is proclaimed as the supreme revelation of God and the ideal for man. In other circles it has been the religious experience of Jesus which is oftenest preached, and men are bidden follow His way of life with God and man. In still other quarters it is His teaching which is dwelt on and men are enlisted as devotees of the Kingdom of God. But the cross, while it is mentioned as a significant unveiling of Jesus' character, or as the most draining ordeal for which He drew on spiritual resources, or as the climax of His devotion to His cause, is seldom preached as a redemptive act. Indeed few of those who have accepted the current liberal theology devote many sermons to the cross of Christ. They feel themselves incapable of treating the theme.

There are various reasons for this. Our exaggerated individualism renders it difficult for us to think of One bearing the sins of others. Our easy optimism makes us think lightly of sin as an obsession of minds which hold unwholesome views of man and of God. Above all, the luxurious circumstances in which modern American Christians have found themselves have dulled our capacities for appreciating sacrifice. We have surrounded ourselves with conveniences and comforts, and we have tried to banish pain.

[4]

The tortured form of One spiked on a beam of wood and done to death does not belong in our mental pictures. Our ideals and manner of life are incompatible with this tragic and heroic symbol. Preachers have felt an unreality in attempting to explore with their people the meaning of the crucifixion.

This neglect of the cross has had something to do with the lack of transforming power in our message. No one can look complacently upon the present condition of our churches. Hundreds of them are barely holding on: they make no gains from the lives about them. In hundreds more, where there is bustle and stir, the activity is about trifles, and lives are not radically altered nor their communities made over. In very few does one find comrades of the conscience of Christ. In most the majority of communicants show no marks of the Lord Jesus in the purposes to which they devote themselves, in their attitudes towards their neighbors, in the opinions which they hold on public questions. Ministers can count on their fingers the number of their people ready to give themselves for an advance of the Kingdom. The wealth in Christian hands in this country is fabulous, but almost all Church Boards are crippled for want of support. More money is taken in at the gates of a single champion prize fight than a million Church members contribute in a whole year to the spread of the Gospel throughout the world. Above all repentance —a fundamental Christian experience—"repentance unto life" as the Westminster divines termed it—is a saving grace seldom seen. That which has most moved other centuries to repentance unto life has been the preaching of Christ crucified. Commenting upon Dwight L. Moody's insistence upon the efficacy of the sacrifice of Christ to do away with sin, Gamaliel Bradford writes:

To some of us, at any rate, whether we can accept this doctrine or not, it seems that the enormous, unparalleled growth and power and majesty of Christianity in the last nineteen hundred years depend upon it.

One would not harshly criticize brethren in the ministry who have shrunk from the word of the cross. We preachers are pitiable men, doomed to be haunted week after week with a sense of the insufficiency of our treatment of subjects obviously too high for us, and on which we are still constrained to speak. We become most abysmally aware of our incompetence when we attempt to set forth the meaning of the suffering and death of the Son of Man. John Milton, who had marvellously celebrated the birth of Jesus in the "Ode on the Morning of Christ's Nativity," attempted a sequel upon the Passion, but after a few exquisite stanzas he ceased in despair, and the fragment is published with the significant note:

This Subject the Author finding to be above the years he had when he wrote it, and nothing satisfied with what was begun, left it unfinished.

And years do not of themselves mature us to deal with this theme. Happily we discover that sermons which seriously try to interpret that supreme event possess a moving power out of proportion to the wisdom of their content.

How are we to preach Christ crucified? We want an interpretation of the cross for our generation which shall move to repentance and faith. In order to remain in close touch with reality, suppose we begin with two questions of history: First, How came it that the Life which subsequent centuries have looked up to as the best ever lived on our earth seemed so intolerable to the dominant groups of His day that they executed Him? Second, Why did Jesus force the issue that made His execution inevitable?

Let us attempt to answer the first question in this initial chapter remembering that we are not attempting a doctrine of the cross for class-room discussion, but for general presentation. How came it that He whom succeeding generations have revered as the best of men was put to death as a criminal? Who were the crucifiers of Christ?

First and foremost the religious leaders whom Church folk respected. It is a tribute to the force conferred by religious conviction that believing men are so often the prime movers in momentous occurrences, both in the blackest crimes and in the brightest triumphs of mankind. Faith, like fire, empowers its possessors whether for woe or for weal. We must not forget that there was ardent faith in God and conscientious loyalty to Him in the Pharisees who contrived the cruel death of our earth's divinest figure. Like one of their own school, they verily thought themselves under compulsion to act as they did.

That is why Church folk should study them carefully. Who were they? The successors of a brave and patriotic company of stalwart believers who had saved the Jewish faith when foreign conquerors attempted to compromise and wreck it by introducing their own customs and worship. They were known for that essential element in vital religion— detachment: they were called Separatists, Pharisees. They were the heirs of a noble army of martyrs. They knew and honored the Bible as the Law of God. They reverenced the scholars who had spent their lives in explaining it and applying it to life. They were the backbone of the synagogues throughout the land. They prayed; they believed in

God's present government of His world and in His immediate control of events. They thought His angelic messengers spoke in the consciences of devout folk and watched for good over their steps. They looked forward to the resurrection of the righteous and their life in the Messiah's everlasting kingdom. They were intense lovers of home and country: in their households there was family religion, and boys, like Saul of Tarsus, were brought up to become devotees and leaders of the Church. They supplied the candidates for the ministry—the scribes who studied and interpreted the Torah. They furnished the missionaries who had enthusiasm to compass sea and land for a single proselyte, and had built up around the synagogues of the whole Mediterranean world companies of the God-fearing who had espoused the faith of Israel.

Men who sincerely try to order their lives by God's will usually work out a system of obligations, to which they hold themselves and seek to hold others. Now some matters can readily be embodied in rules—keeping the Sabbath, observing sacred festivals and fasts, adopting methodical times and habits of prayer, setting aside a tenth of one's gains for religious purposes. And some matters cannot be thus codified—having clean thoughts and generous sympathies, being conciliatory, honoring every human being, however unadmirable, as kin to God, serving him as his heavenly Father understandingly cares for him. And matters which can be incorporated in rules tend to be stressed above those which cannot be precisely defined. And when men have their beliefs and duties clearly stated, and are earnestly living by them, they are not apt to distinguish between more and less important items in their religious code: all of it is precious to them. They do not wish any of it changed. Sincere religion is inherently conservative. It deals with tested values.

Jesus scandalized them by disregarding practices which they considered God's Law. He broke the Sabbath shockingly. When asked to speak in the synagogues, His addresses upset many in the congregation. He associated with disreputable people—with loose women and with unpatriotic profiteering farmers of revenue. He touched the academic pride of their scholars: how should a carpenter correct their explanation of Scriptures which they had spent their lives in studying and for which they had the authority of recognized experts? Many of them had never heard Him for themselves, and at second or tenth hand, when the intervening hands are unfriendly, His sayings and doings appeared even more insufferable. From the outset He was surrounded in their minds with an atmosphere of suspicion. They sent spies to watch Him, and spies have a way of hearing what they fancy they are sent to hear. The Pharisees felt themselves guardians of the faith of Israel. Their fathers had fought and bled for it; their own lives were wrapped up in it; they were holding it in the dark days of Roman dominion for their children and children's children. Could they allow this Innovator, this Charlatan who made preposterous claims for Himself, to go on deceiving simple folk and perhaps wreck the Church? Quite apart from the embittering encounters Jesus had with some of them—encounters which may have been colored in our gospels by the subsequent strife between the Synagogue and the growing Christian Church, there was enough difference between His faith and life and theirs to rouse determined antagonism. In loyalty to God they must put an end to His mischievous career.

A second group were the inheritors of a lucrative commercial privilege—the aristocratic Sadducean priests who controlled the Temple area. They also were churchmen, but in comparison with the Pharisees, their religion was a subordinate and moderate interest. It was an inheritance which they cherished with an antiquarian's regard for its more primitive form. Their thought of Deity was of a remote and unaggressive Being, who left men to work out their own affairs, who certainly did not interfere or help by sending angelic spirits. God wished from Israel a seemly recognition in the maintenance of the time-honored ceremonies. For the rest they were broad-minded. Their predecessors had welcomed the culture and customs of the Greeks, and they probably had a much more

tolerant attitude in religion than the Pharisees. One might have picked up a Greek poem
or drama in their homes; they were interested
in the on-goings of the larger world; and
after the manner of cultivated liberals they
smiled in superior fashion on the narrow pre-
occupations of scribes with the details of the
religious code. They were much more concerned with politics and finance than with religion. So long as Jesus remained in Galilee,
they may never have heard of Him; or if
some rumor of Him came to their ears, they
would pay little attention to it. The alarm of
the Pharisees over His teaching would have
seemed to them a petty squabble which was
no concern of theirs.

But when Jesus invaded the Temple pre-
cincts and created a commotion by overturn-
ing the tables of the money-changers, these
gentlemen were roused. Here was a dangerous social Radical. Doubtless their leasing
of space for booths in the outer court of the
Temple had been criticized before, and there
was popular talk over the prices of doves and
lambs, and grumbling at the rate of exchange

for the half-shekel. But this was the usual proletarian murmuring. Did they not provide a public convenience in these business arrangements? Were they not assisting worshippers in their religious duties? Did not the ancient Law clearly enjoin that the Temple tax should be paid in a particular coin? And must not someone supply facilities for exchanging the various currencies which pilgrims brought with them from all over the Empire for the proper silver piece? Was not four per cent a moderate broker's fee for such an exchange? The idea of this upcountry Agitator appearing and, without a word to anybody in authority, making this disturbance in the Temple court, and infecting the populace with the absurd notion that there should be no charge for perfectly legitimate ecclesiastical business! Where did He think animals for sacrifice would be procured? What did He consider a reasonable charge for exchange, if He called four per cent robbery? Who was He, anyhow, to take upon Himself to reform the financial methods of men whose forebears had derived their incomes unquestioned from these leases? His attack was a reflection not only upon them, but upon their honored fathers. Annas and Caiaphas had never seen the court of the Temple without booths and stalls; it was to them part of the natural order of things that cattle and doves should be sold there and money exchanged. Further they had been born to the tradition that the sacred area of the Temple belonged to the hereditary priesthood, and that they were to derive their support from its ceremonies. How could they understand the indignant feelings of Jesus? The charge, which the false witnesses brought, that He had threatened to destroy the Temple, may have had some slight basis in fact. Such statements are seldom made out of whole cloth. Jesus may have expressed the feeling that, if this Temple made with hands were destroyed, real religion might not lose much. That would disturb these gentlemen in their family sentiment, in their inherited faith, in their economic interests.

And they were politicians with a keen eye for the political situation. At the moment they were on fair terms with the Roman Empire and were allowed some freedom in the management of local affairs. A demagogue of this sort, as Caiaphas remarked, might stir up a political mess, and embroil them with the Roman authorities. Could they risk allowing Him to go on?*

A third figure among the crucifiers is the representative of imperialistic government. He seems to have been impressed by Jesus— more impressed than the scribes or the priests. We pity him as part of a system which our age feels to be inherently faulty. In theory at least we do not believe in one people governing another. It is bad for both peoples. It creates such attitudes as one sees in this scene—the priests fawning upon the governor and Pilate overbearing toward them

*Doctor L. P. Jacks has said of our contemporary churches: "The gravamen of the charge against the Church is not so much that there are definite abuses in its corporate life as that there is a general atmosphere of acquiescence in all that is worldly and conventional. No one knows exactly what ideal of life the Church stands for, unless that it is that of a kindly and good-natured toleration of things as they are, with a mild desire that they may grow better in time, so far as that is compatible with the maintenance of existing vested interests." That is the position of the Sadducee; and Jesus touched it at its most sensitive point when He assailed vested interests.

and insulting the nation by the derisive title he orders nailed above the Victim on the cross. But among imperialistic peoples few have understood their business as well as the Romans. They probably kept Judæa in better order than any native leader could have kept it. They governed brutally, but there are still many who think that inferiors must be made to know their place. Jesus had been struck with their haughty attitude: "Ye know that the rulers of the Gentiles lord it." It may have been partially a patriot's unwillingness to speak against His own countrymen before an overlord which sealed His lips in the judgment hall.

All our narratives agree that the governor was most reluctant to execute this Prisoner. He suggested expedient after expedient to obviate it. He tried everything except the direct course of following his conscience and seeking to deal justly towards the Man before him. The system of which he was a part entangled him. Rome asked her procurators to keep the tribute flowing steadily from their provinces and to maintain quiet. No gov-

ernor wished complaints lodged against him
with his superiors. Pilate had to live with
these priests, and in the end it seemed easier
to let them have their way with this Peasant
from Galilee. He was poor and insignificant,
and to this day justice is never the same for
the unfriended sons of poverty as for the
wealthy and influential. Paul, claiming his
rights as a Roman citizen, was to have days
in court his Master could not command.

To the last Pilate was uncomfortable about
the case. He did his best to shift responsibility—on Herod, on the crowd, on the
priests. But the priests knew their man and
played skilfully upon his loyalties and his
fears. The fourth evangelist makes them
say: "If thou release this man, thou art not
Cæsar's friend." Fidelity to Cæsar was both
a Roman's patriotism and his religion. They
were appealing to Pilate's principles, and they
won their point. Pilate washed his hands,
but throughout the centuries his name has
been coupled with this event as responsible
for it on the lips of thousands who repeat
"crucified under Pontius Pilate."

A fourth figure among the crucifiers, although he is hardly a decisive factor, is a
man of the gay world—Herod Antipas. A
scion of an able family, born to wealth and
position, brought up in Rome at the imperial
court, admitted to the fashionable society of
the capital in the golden age of Augustus, a
member of the smart set, he knew all about
the latest delicacies of the table, had a keen
eye for a beautiful dancer, and surrounded by
boon companions lived for pleasure. Like
many in similar circumstances in contemporary America he had a shabby marital record,
having become infatuated with his half-
brother's wife, for whom he divorced his own
wife, and whom he stole from her husband.
But divorces even of this sordid variety were
not bad form then, any more than they are
among ourselves to-day, and bad form was
the only taboo Herod revered. He had a rep-
utation for political shrewdness, and he had
burnt his fingers in handling one prophet,
John, and was wary of repeating the blunder.
Jesus dreaded what He called "the leaven of
Herod"—loose morals, lavish outlay and

sharp politics. He had spoken of this tetrarch as "that fox." Now these two were
face to face.

Herod displayed a man of the world's ver-
satility in asking Him "many questions"—
one wonders what they were. He was clever
and was pleased to display his knowledge of
religious fine points before his companions
and before the priests. It was a chance to
impress them. But Herod could make nothing of Jesus. And Jesus could make nothing
of Herod. He had borne witness to his Messiahship before Caiaphas and the Sanhedrin;
He had admitted His kingship to Pontius Pilate; but He had not a syllable to utter to
Antipas. The tetrarch had heard of Him as
a wonder-worker and craved the chance to
see Him do something startling. But Jesus'
mighty works are not tricks to entertain and
astonish. Herod had a conscience; could not
Jesus appeal to that with some piercing story
such as Nathan told adulterous David? Did
the Saviour ever confront a needier sinner?
But He had not a word for him.

Herod was apparently "past feeling," and

Jesus gave him up. This clownish roysterer and his cronies could think of nothing to do with their disappointing Prisoner but tog Him out in mock finery and make game of Him. Fancy the mind of Jesus while this went on! It cost Pilate some struggle to condemn Him; but when He was sent away from the tetrarch's palace, Herod had been laughing at Him as a buffoon, and was now smiling at his own shrewdness in outwitting the governor, and handing his awkward case back to him.

A fifth figure among the crucifiers is a disillusioned idealist. We have no reason to think that the man of Kerioth did not enlist in the cause of Jesus from the same high motives as the other disciples. If anything, it was harder for him, the only Judæan in the group, than for Galileans. He heard all that they heard and he shared all that they shared; and, like them, he was disappointed. He had looked for a different issue. Jesus outdistanced his ideals; he fancied that Jesus did not measure up to his ideals, and he grew critical. With many the attempt "to go beyond themselves and wind themselves too high" is followed by a reaction. What he had hoped for, and hoped for immediately, did not happen, and Judas became bitter. He felt himself duped. The confident attitude of Jesus as He set His face to what seemed to Judas folly and defeat, irritated him. He was no longer the reasonable man he had been. It was that, perhaps, which led the disciples in retrospect to recall that the devil entered into him. They felt that he was at war with himself. And in such plight men not infrequently turn on those to whom they have been most warmly attached. Their disgust with themselves they are apt to vent on those who make them uncomfortable. Iago says of Cassio: "He hath a daily beauty in his life that makes me ugly." Jesus became hateful to Judas Iscariot. There may be a shred of truth in the theories which make his betrayal of the Master an attempt to force His hand, and compel Him to assume his power.

For what was it that Judas betrayed to the priests? Obviously not merely the spot where their police could arrest Jesus. That was not worth paying for. The police could follow Him and find out His haunts. Probably Judas betrayed, as many modern interpreters think, the secret of Jesus' Messiahship, which was talked of in the inner circle but not published abroad. That was not clear to the priests or to the public even after the entry amid hosannas, for the shouts of a crowd are not evidence. Now they had a basis for a trial, so Judas was in a sense forcing Jesus to declare Himself. But our narratives imply that Judas did it vindictively, not affectionately.

Disillusioned idealists become sour and cynical. And in cynicism consciences unravel: Judas may easily have grown careless in handling the money in his custody. Avarice cannot have been the main motive in the betrayal, but greed has a place in most ignoble stories. Very trifling sums induce people still to hideous crimes. When a man is embittered, he is capable of anything, and it was a cynic who drove the shabby bargain with the chief priests and went out with thirty pieces of silver jingling in his purse and a betrayed Master on his conscience.

A sixth factor among the crucifiers is a crowd. The individuals who composed it were decent men, kind to their families and neighbors, and personally they would not have been cruel to this Prophet from Galilee. They had a prejudice against Him, and that prejudice was worked up until they were fused into a howling mob. In such a mass a man is lifted out of himself, loses control of his feelings, and his passions surge unchecked and augmented by the passions of the throng around him. He becomes a thousand times himself emotionally. Shakespeare's Bassanio speaks of

The buzzing pleasèd multitude
Whose every something being blent together
Turns to a wild of nothing save of joy.

And the reverse is true when the crowd is prejudiced and their every something being blent together turns to a wild of nothing save of cruelty.

A crowd, being emotionally intense, is very suggestible. A catchword will set it off. Our propagandists and advertisers have taught us

[25]

how we can be worked on in masses by names, phrases, pictures. And crowds are much more readily suggestible to the more primitive and coarser sentiments than to the finer. Man is a thinly varnished savage at best, lump him together in throngs and the varnish melts at the touch. When Pilate appeared unwilling to grant the priests' request, the crowd was swayed by nationalism; the priests were their own, and the governor the representative of the hated oppressor. They had a traditional right to claim clemency for a prisoner at the Passover. They will use it, and natural self-assertion impels them not to ask for One whom Pilate would gladly let them have. A suggestion is given them—Barabbas, a popular revolutionary of the crude type—a slogan for the emotions of a crowd.

Jesus can hardly have been popular. How much better "copy" for our own press Barabbas would be than the Teacher of Nazareth! Besides Barabbas is the nationalistic type Pilate would least like to release. Mobs feel and scarcely think. Could these men as individuals have calmly weighed Jesus and

Barabbas, the result might have been different; but they were atingle with their cruder instincts. And a crowd which takes to shouting works itself to a violent pitch, and when thwarted can become fiendishly brutal. The spectators who packed the tiers of the Coliseum, turned down their thumbs at some fallen gladiator and yelled themselves hoarse demanding his death, would not have done anything of the sort by themselves. Each man in the crowd has lost his sense of personal responsibility. It is what men do in a social set, a political party, an economic group, a nation, a religious assembly, that is likely to be least moral and most diabolically savage. Pilate did his weak best not to execute Jesus; Herod found loutish amusement in Him, but showed no desire for His blood; Judas wished Him out of his way, but jail would have satisfied him; the crowd, with their tribal feelings roused—the instincts of the hunting pack—shouted "Crucify Him, crucify Him!"

A seventh factor among the crucifiers was a guard of soldiers. Jesus never spoke harshly of the military profession. One of His rare compliments was paid to an officer who had expressed his faith in terms of soldierly obedience. And probably it was in extenuation of the legionaries charged with the grim details of His execution that He prayed: "Father, forgive them, for they know not what they do." But it was by men prepared for their task by military discipline that He was done to death at Golgotha.

That system is deliberately planned to depersonalize those whom it trains. They are educated not to decide for themselves, but to give machine-like response to a command. Such a system, while it has noble associations with courage, loyalty, honor and self-efface-ment, counteracts that which Christianity tries hardest to create—a reasoning con-science. The soldiers who scourged Jesus and spiked His hands and feet to the beams of the cross never thought what they were doing—they were victims of a discipline which had crucified their moral judgments.

Their occupation was held in high honor as the typical and most essential patriotic service. Rome ruled by physical might. She believed in awing inferior peoples and encouraged her soldiers to strike terror into them. The scourging which Pilate ordered—"the terrible preface," as it was called, to capital punishment—was forbidden for Roman citizens, but it was customary for provincials. A small guard was ordered to inflict on Jesus this appalling indignity in public—stripping Him, binding Him to a stake in a stooping position with hands behind Him, and beating Him with thongs at the ends of which were leaden balls or sharp-pointed bones.

And when that prostrating ordeal was over they took Him for further maltreatment to the privacy of the guardroom. Brutal mockery of the condemned was allowed the soldiers in order to maintain their *morale*. All the finer feelings must be overcome in those whose trade is iron and blood. And privacy seems to be an inevitable temptation to men with fellow-beings in their power. Schoolboys, jailors, keepers of the weak in mind or body, generation after generation, have to be watched against outbreaks of savagery to their victims. It was expected of the soldiers —a crude comic interlude to their rough day. But in fairness to these systematically hardened men let us recall that when the Prisoner was uplifted on the cross, slowly bleeding to death in agony, educated and revered religious leaders, professors of divinity, vented their detestation of Him with gibes. Theological animosity renders men as callous as professional hangmen.

Perhaps more so, for these soldiers had to restrain themselves from feeling by gambling at the foot of the cross. They had to sit by while the crucified writhed, and groaned, and cried, in their prolonged misery. It is not surprising that they resorted to the excitement of playing dice as a mental relief. They are typical representatives of callings into which men cannot put themselves—their minds and consciences and hearts. Such callings rob those who engage in them of moral vitality and make them fit agents of tragic occurrences like Calvary.

But there is still an eighth factor without which the crucifixion would not have taken place—the public. Behind the chief actors in the drama at Golgotha we see thousands of obscure figures—the populace of the city. One fancies them getting up in the morning and hearing rumors of a case on before the governor. The city, crowded with Passover pilgrims, would be more excitable and talkative than usual, and news of events at the palace, involving the Sanhedrin, would spread rapidly. Then, as people were in the midst of their morning's work, they would catch sight of that sinister procession tramping through the streets on the way to the place of execution outside the city wall. We can overhear such remarks as "Hello! another hanging to-day? Who's to be hung? Those two bandits? Who's the third prisoner? That Prophet from Galilee? Oh, they got Him very quickly, didn't they?" And as prisoners and guards filed past, the day's work was resumed.

Behind all earth's tragedies there is a public whose state of mind has much to do with the central event. Even under the least democratic government the authorities dare not go more than a certain distance without the

popular will. The thousands of uncaring no-
bodies, to whom what was done with Jesus
was a matter of indifference, gave scribes and
priests and governor their chance. These obscure folk felt themselves without responsibility. What had they to do with this Prophet
from the north country who had ridden into
the city, hailed by a crowd of provincial pilgrims? Possibly it was of them that Jesus
was thinking—the public of the capital city—
when He said: "O Jerusalem, Jerusalem, that
killeth the prophets."

The public is never of one mind; it represents various shades of opinion and feeling—
sympathetic, hostile, indifferent; and all shades
were there in Jerusalem. But if enough of
its inhabitants had really cared about Jesus,
He would never have been crucified. The
chief handicap of the public is ignorance. The
mass of the dwellers in Jerusalem knew next
to nothing about the Prophet from Galilee.
But Jesus did not weep over them merely because of their lack of information. Religious
capitals, like cathedral towns, are proverbially
hard to move. Religion was an old story to

those who lived in the neighborhood of the venerable Temple and were familiar with the figures of the great doctors of the Law. They were complacent in sacred traditions of the past and not open to fresh incomings of the Most High. Jesus wept over their apathy. To Him it seemed that even unfeeling stones must respond to One who so manifestly represented God. They did not know the things which belonged to peace because they did not wish to know them. Jerusalem slew the Son of God not only because He had won the sharp ill-will of the powerful few, but also because the many did not want to be bothered with Him. And the public of Jerusalem, who thought the fate of this Stranger none of their business, had to bear the doom with their as-yet-unborn children; for judgment brings home social obligations and convinces us that by a myriad unsuspected cords men are tied up in one bundle of life in cities, in nations, in races and in a world of men. These thousands of citizens of Jerusalem never went through the form of washing their hands, like Pilate. They were unaware or any accountability for this execution. But history with its destruction of the city rendered its verdict upon them.

Such a survey of the factors which crucified Jesus—and a course rather than a single sermon is obviously necessary to treat them with sufficient explicitness—forces men to think. This was the world which executed the Life subsequent generations until this hour revere as the best earth has seen. And plainly it is the world in which we still live. All these forces are present and active in our society—religious intolerance, commercial privilege, political expediency, pleasure-loving irresponsibility, unfaithfulness, the mob spirit, militarism, public apathy. These are perennial evils. They are deep-seated in the very structure of human society. The forms of political and economic and ecclesiastical organization may alter, but these remain under all forms. We should find them in a socialist republic or a communist state, as surely as in an imperial despotism or a capitalist régime. Moreover they act and react upon each other.

The priests help Judas to his treachery and incite the mob; Pilate stimulates the priests to play politics; the political methods of both governor and religious leaders keep the public morally indifferent; their sinister motives interweave into a corporate force for evil. Together they make up what Jesus called "the power of darkness," the satanic kingdom.

It is significant that the national and ecclesiastical capital is the slayer of the prophets. Evil organizes itself with this inherent solidarity and possesses a group—a church, a nation, a race. These forces were present in the villages and towns of Galilee, but they came to a focus where the organization of the Jewish Church and the Jewish nation had its seat, and where the representative of imperial government exercised his power. Wickedness is a racial force. It propagates itself generation after generation. Jesus recognized the unity of the factors with which He was struggling with similar factors, which had always been present in the life of His people, when He spoke of this generation which was crucifying Him having upon it "all the righteous blood shed on earth," from the blood of Abel on the first pages of the Jewish Bible to the blood of Zachariah recorded on its last pages. Evil spreads itself laterally, building up a corporate force of wickedness, and passes itself on from age to age, linking the generations in a solidarity of sin.

When we examine the factors which slew Jesus, we recognize them at once as contemporaries. We can attach modern names to them. There is nothing abnormal or unusual about these men who rear the cross: they are acting true to type—a type which recurs century after century throughout history. They are average folk. We must not blacken their characters. John Stuart Mill, whose ethical judgments are singularly dispassionate, says of them:

They were not worse than men commonly are, but rather the contrary, men who possessed in a full, or somewhat more than a full measure the religious, moral and patriotic feelings of their people; the very kind of men who in all times, our own included, have every chance of passing through life blameless and unspotted.

[36]

We can think of no more high-minded young man than the student of Gamaliel, Saul of Tarsus, and we know how cordially he approved the course taken by the leaders of Israel in putting Jesus out of the way.

We can easily multiply from history and literature men far more villainous—a Cæsar Borgia or an Iago for instance. Indeed we can find more depraved figures in almost any community, if we look for them. But the purpose of Jesus and the purposes of even good people clash. The inevitableness of the crucifixion is brought home to us. The issue between the motives of Jesus and those of the mass of mankind is thrown into light. They are irreconcilable. Life is a desperately real struggle between mutually destroying forces. If the motives of Jesus prevail, the factors that slew Him will cease to be. If the motives of Caiaphas and Pilate, of the mob, the soldiers and the public prevail—there is an execution: "Away with such a fellow from the earth."

There are three crosses on Calvary: on two of them society is trying to rid itself of predatory bandits, on the third it placed One whom it considered also its enemy, perhaps a worse enemy since He was placed on the central cross. We level up with our standards of right, and we also level down. He who is above the conscience of the community is as likely to be slain as he who is below. This is our world; this is the society in which we move; these are the types of people with whom we associate; this is the public to which we belong. The slayers of Jesus are our relatives, kinsmen in thought and feeling. A sense of complicity in what they did comes upon us. We are bound up with them in this bundle of human life. The corporate evil which dominated first-century Palestine and moved these men to kill their Best dominates our world and is compassing similar fell results. Trails of blood lead to our doors. Wretched men that we are, who shall deliver us out of this social body of death?

And these factors are not only about us, they are also within us. As we scan these men who sent Jesus to His death—devout Pharisee and conservative Sadducee, Roman politician and false friend, emotional mob and unthinking soldiers, the host of indifferent or approving faces of the public behind them—their motives and feelings have been and are our own. You may recall in Hawthorne's "Mosses from an Old Manse" the scene where going through the virtuoso's collection, he nearly falls over a huge bundle, like a peddler's pack, done up in sackcloth and very securely strapped and corded. "It is Christian's burden of sin," said the virtuoso. "O pray, let me see it, cried I. For many a year I have longed to know its contents." "Look into your own conscience and memory," replied the virtuoso. "You will there find a list of whatever it contained." It is so with the motives of those who planned and carried out the death of Jesus. We do not need to ask: "Lord, is it I?" We are aware of belonging in this same realm of darkness, and of having dealt with His brethren very much as He was dealt with. As we think of ourselves, we shudder —"God, be merciful to me, a sinner."

Men speak of the absence of the sense of sin in our time. It has never been vigorous in any age, save as some judgment of history or the disturbing presence of the ideal has created it. We have witnessed a judgment on a colossal scale in the World War—a judgment upon our entire civilization. Some of us said to ourselves, feeling mankind in the grip of overmastering social forces of passion and greed and brutality: "Now is your hour and the power of darkness." And we know ourselves a long way yet from redemption from the motives which brought it on. Underneath the ease and comfort of our day there is restless discontent. Some of it is crassly materialistic—the common envy of the have-nots for the haves, the craving of the have-littles to have more. But souls are never satisfied with things. Life is in relationships, human and divine, in purposes. And men are dissatisfied with the quality of life. To take them to Calvary and show them the factors which nailed Jesus on the cross is to uncover for them a far more terrible world than they dreamed they were in, and to uncover for them themselves.

This gives us an inkling of Jesus' reason

for putting Himself into men's hands and letting them do with Him as they would. His broken and bleeding body on the cross is the exposure of a murderous world. The Crucified becomes one with the unrecognized and misused and cruelly treated in every age. The nail-pierced Figure on Calvary haunts our race as a symbol of what is forever taking place generation after generation, and of what each of us has his part in.

Readers of Ibsen's drama "Emperor and Galilean" will recall how Julian is made to ask—

Where is He now? Has He been at work elsewhere since that happened at Golgotha?

I dreamed of Him lately. I dreamed that I had subdued the whole world. I ordained that the memory of the Galilean should be rooted out on earth; and it was rooted out. Then the spirits came and ministered to me, and bound wings on my shoulders, and I soared aloft into infinite space, till my feet rested on another world.

It was another world than mine. Its curve was vaster, its light more golden, and many moons circled around it. Then I looked down

at my own earth—the Emperor's earth that I
had made Galileanless—and I thought that all
that I had done was very good.

But behold there came a procession by me
on the strange earth where I stood. There
were soldiers and judges and executioners at
the head of it and weeping women followed.
And lo, in the midst of the slow-moving ar-
ray, was the Galilean, alive and bearing a
cross on His back. Then I called to Him and
said, "Whither away, Galilean?" And He
turned His face to me and smiled, nodded
slowly and said, "To the place of the skull."

Where is He now? What if that at Golgotha, near Jerusalem, was but a wayside matter, a thing done as it were in passing! What
if He goes on and on, and suffers and dies,
and conquers, again and again, from world to
world!

It is a vivid way of picturing the solidarity
of the worlds of every generation, each offering its Golgotha. It is there that men come to
themselves and realize their plight and the
plight of society. Walter Pater said that "the
way to perfection is through a series of disgusts." To let men see the factors which enact the tragedy outside the wall of Jerusalem

is to disgust them with their world and with themselves. If some protest that this is not a wholesome state of mind, one may answer in the words of that robust thinker, Walter Bagehot: "So long as men are very imperfect, a sense of great imperfection should cleave to them." It is a necessary part of the process towards genuine healthy-mindedness. When they realize what caused the torture and execution of Jesus, they cry, "O not that! Such a world is intolerable!" And made conscious that they are builders of such worlds, and that their hands are stained, they hunger and thirst after righteousness.

WHY DID HE HAVE HIMSELF
CRUCIFIED?

CHAPTER II

IN our last chapter we raised the question, how came it that He whom subsequent ages have revered as the Best our earth has known was publicly executed by the authorities of His Church and nation and world? We studied the factors which combined to crucify Jesus, and we saw in His death an exposure of our race, an uncovering of forces of evil which appear with appalling repetition century after century in human society. The tragedy of Golgotha is a shocking revelation of what is in man. As such it disgusts us with ourselves and our world, and stirs us to want to become different, and to welcome any power which can make us different.

But is the death of Jesus just one more instance of the fate which awaits men ahead of or above their contemporaries? Many other occurrences expose for us the wickedness of mankind. Is "Christ's blood just another

murder"? Why did Jesus court death by going up to the capital and forcing Himself upon
the attention of rulers whom He knew to be
hostile? And when His death was imminent
why did He shrink from it, and pray for some
other issue to His career?

The various lives of Christ which have appeared in the past hundred years answer dif-
ferently the question why He went to Calvary. You will think of several of these
answers from divers schools of interpretation
—those who have envisaged Him as a social
revolutionary, a martyred teacher, an apoca-
lyptic visionary, a religious genius. In arriving at an answer it is obviously necessary
to distinguish in the narratives between material which can be traced back with some assurance to Jesus Himself and material which
is due to the reflection of His followers subsequent to His death and resurrection. In
our preaching we do not wish to cumber sermons with details of Biblical criticism; but
we must form some opinion of the historical
facts, and then attempt the delicate task of
trying to fathom our Lord's own mind as He

thought upon the issue of His work. We may not reach assured conclusions, but we must try to understand His motives, for without such appreciative sympathy we cannot enter for ourselves or lead others into intelligent fellowship with Him in His sufferings.

In answering the question, Why did Jesus go to the cross? we may start with this statement of apparently indisputable fact: that His journey to Jerusalem was deliberately planned,* that He foresaw the peril involved, and that up to the very last He was of two minds as to the event—He prayed for escape from the terrible ordeal of a violent death, and He accepted it as His Father's will for Him, explaining it as the Divine method of

*"We are ruthless with the story, rejecting miracle, pious legend, everything in which we cannot believe. One fact remains. Do what we will to the story as we have it, there is a moment when His face is set to go to Jerusalem—to proclaim the new truth, to die proclaiming it. He went—no one understood why He was going; He died—no one understood why He died. The historical criticism which would destroy that part of the story is negligible. He deliberately died for His belief, and died for mankind. I have tried to shake that certainty: I have played the devil's advocate against my own exceeding great desire, knowing that I cannot afford to build upon a lie, however dear. The death, the decision and the purpose of the death of Jesus stand firm. It *was* so." (J. Middleton Murry, "Things to Come," p. 109. *By permission of The Macmillan Company, publishers.*)

achieving His purpose.' What, then, was in His mind when He thought of His death as a means of furthering God's kingdom? What induced Him to leave Galilee and bring on the conflict at the capital?

We can best begin at the first public event in His career—the baptism at the Jordan. In John Jesus heard the prophet who embodied the finest conscience of his race. He was shaking the nation with his preaching—priests and teachers—respected leaders of the public; soldiers, tax-farmers, harlots—the classes outside the social pale; masses of the common folk with whom religion becomes a passion only at rare intervals. Here were hundreds disclosing their inward wants and shames and longings. If later an evangelist speaks of Jesus as moved with compassion for the multitudes, this was doubtless the first occasion on which He had seen throngs in an attitude of spirit which would move Him. And how did they affect Him? One might suppose that His first impulse would be to join John in preaching to them. He agreed with John's message in large part; He was to begin His own ministry by repeating its main call; but He was not moved to preach. His instant impulse was to place Himself beside these penitent people, to share their baptism of repentance, to confess with them the sins of Israel.

Throughout the centuries Christians have been puzzled by Jesus' insistence on undergoing this symbol of repentance. What did He have on His conscience to confess? Our crass individualism hinders our understanding Him. If His nation was not fulfilling God's purpose, He was implicated in its failure. If the leaders of the Church were there, acknowledging its faultiness and their guilt, He as a member of the Church was involved in its sin. If social outcasts, harlots and publicans, were there, pouring out their penitence, He was accountable for conditions which helped make harlots and grasping collectors of revenue. If common folk of all sorts were there, baring their soiled souls and dedicating themselves to a new life, they were His kinsmen and He belonged with them, sharing their abasement and their hunger and thirst after righteousness. It was no pose on His part when He put Himself at their side as a penitent. .

Other sensitive spirits have found themselves entering into the experiences of fellow-creatures. You may recall Walt Whitman's poem on a fugitive slave hunted down by a mounted posse with dogs:

The hounded slave that flags in the race, leans
    by the fence, blowing, cover'd with
    sweat,
The twinges that sting like needles his legs
    and neck, the murderous buckshot and
    the bullets—
All these I feel or am.
I am the hounded slave, I wince at the bite of
    the dogs;
Hell and despair are upon me, crack and again
    crack the marksmen;
I clutch the rails of the fence, my gore dribs,
    thinn'd with the ooze of my skin;
I fall on the weeds and stones.
The riders spur their unwilling horses, haul
    close,
Taunt my dizzy ears and beat me violently
    over the head with whip stocks.
Agonies are one of my changes of garments.

I do not ask the wounded person how he feels;
    I myself become the wounded person;
My hurts turn livid upon me as I lean on a
    cane and observe.

And with Jesus it is more than poetic sympathy which identifies Him with the experiences of others. He had that sympathy to a
marked degree as His parables attest. He
puts Himself into His characters and makes
us sense the feelings of the prodigal in the
far country and the unemployed laborers
waiting tediously in the market-place. But
this goes deeper than poetic sympathy: His
conscience acknowledges responsibility for the
community's wrong. Mr. Hutton tells us that
F. D. Maurice felt "a sort of self-reproachful
complicity in every sinful tendency of his
age." Professor Josiah Royce once said that
when he met a wooden mind, he felt bitterly
ashamed "that he lived in a world where
truth could be made so dull and uninterest-
ing." The Lord's Prayer is recorded as
taught by Jesus to His disciples; it sounds as
though He had prayed it with them. He who
underwent the baptism of repentance may

well have joined in praying "Forgive us our debts." He was implicated in the sins of society.

The first evangelist stresses the contrast at this point between Jesus and John. John's conscience was burdened with the sins of the nation, and with flaming words he called on sinful people to repent. Jesus' conscience was burdened both with the sins of the nation and with the sense of His complicity in these sins. One catches a rebuke in His saying to the Baptist, when the latter objects to baptizing Him: "Suffer it now, for thus it becometh us—thee and Me and every God-loving man and woman—to fulfil all righteousness."

In the noble words of his second inaugural, Mr. Lincoln set the North and South side by side as jointly chargeable with the institution of human slavery in our land, and as jointly sharing the horror of the civil strife in God's judgment on that iniquitous social wrong. "God gives to both North and South this terrible war, as the woe due to those by whom the offense came." Lincoln was criticized at the time by the self-righteous in the North who believed that all the guilt belonged with those who had been upholding the institution of slavery. But it was he, and not his critics, who shared the conscience of Jesus. Jesus saw sin bringing in its wake inevitable doom —"the wrath to come" of which John thundered; He felt Himself compromised in the godlessness of His people; He stood with the conscience-awakened group who confessed their sins and dedicated themselves to bring in social righteousness.

At the Baptism the evangelists report that Jesus heard a Divine Voice speaking to Him. The words in which this message came to Him are variously recorded; but the earliest narrative phrases it in language taken from the second part of the Book of Isaiah. This was a favorite section of Scripture with Jesus. Evidently He had been thinking of His career in the light of the prophet's picture of the Servant of the Lord. When He placed Himself beside the company of His penitent fellow-countrymen, and received with them the symbol of repentance and cleansing, this Voice sounded clearly in His conscience. He knew Himself God's Son, His Servant in whom He delights.

There is still a difference of opinion among scholars whether Jesus Himself thought of His death in terms of the fifty-third chapter of Isaiah. Apart altogether from the weight we may lay upon reminiscences of the language of that chapter in certain of His sayings as we now have them, it seems unbelievable that He could dwell on the picture of the Servant of the Lord, as the prophet draws it, finding the ideal for Himself more clearly here than anywhere else in Scripture, and omit the tragic conclusion of the Servant's career. If so much duller minds as His disciples found Jesus in this portrait after His death, it is very difficult to think that He did not look often at this picture as the probable conclusion of His life's work.

At the Jordan He showed Himself unmistakably in fullest accord with this prophetic ideal: He enters vicariously into the sins of the community, confessing them with the penitent group. A profound New Testament writer sees that in this act Jesus began His

Saviourhood: "This is He that came by water." We speak of a man's "arriving" in his
chosen calling, or "coming to his own" in
public influence. This writer sees Jesus arriving at His sway over men's lives "by
water"—by His fineness of conscience which
recognized the need for social redemption and
which shared His brethren's repentance and
dedication to righteousness. He does not
come by water only, our writer at once adds
"and by blood." He joins the Baptism and
the Crucifixion. We are following his insight when we have begun to try to interpret
Jesus' motives in having Himself crucified by
studying His conscience in taking part in this
act of corporate repentance.

Then follows the Temptation, the inevitable reaction from an experience of spiritual
exaltation—a solitary struggle in which Jesus
faces this newly-espoused ideal for His career
with the opinions held by the best folk of His
day concerning the course God's Representative should take. No one knew better than
He that the battlefield where a man wins or
loses is within himself. He carried every

broken commandment—a murder, infidelity to a marriage vow, an unclean life—back to a wrong thought. Our current psychology with its stress upon images reminds us that it is the picture of himself in a child's mind or the picture of a nation in the minds of its citizens which determines destiny. Perhaps it was this all-important conflict of pictures in the popular mind of which the poet, William Blake, was thinking—and few have more concerned themselves with images than he— when he penned the familiar lines:

> I will not cease from *mental* fight,
>   Nor shall my sword sleep in my hand,
> Till we have set Jerusalem
>   In England's green and pleasant land.

The holy city descends from God out of heaven, but it enters earth through pictures in minds which become devotees of an ideal.

Jesus looked at the pictures which the best people of His time were drawing of the methods by which God's kingdom was to come. It is significant that one of these pictures is taken from the Bible. If they had not been noble ideals, they would have possessed no appeal for Him. The three parables in which He has portrayed His own spiritual struggle (for ultimately they are autobiography and go back to Him) describe perennial temptations which we can all understand. With His unusual capacities, let Him devote Himself to men's primary physical needs, and render them that substantial help. Or with His assured faith, let Him attempt something spectacular which shall gain Him publicity as accredited of God, and so capture men's imagination and confidence. Or with His practical knowledge of the world, let Him ally Himself with the ruling powers of the age, and so procure backing for His spiritual purpose. Considerations of humanity, of religion, of common sense, presented themselves to Him. His penetrating discernment heard in them diabolic solicitations. These suggestions proposed matters for which He longed both for Himself and for others—healthy physical conditions, a faith which wrought wonders, the kingdoms of the world and their glory in literature, art, science, national characteristics, made part of the commonwealth of God. But He refused to pursue any of them directly: He will be God's Servant to bring spiritual emancipation by becoming one with His brethren in their needs and obligations and by His conscientiousness to waken their loyalty to God and man.

Next we pass to the scene at Cæsarea Philippi. There Jesus asks His closest friends to tell Him what people think of Him. He has been doing His work, He has won followers, He has achieved some results; He will face His career again through the opinions of others. Like most friends, His disciples do not tell Him the worst people were saying about Him. His relatives thought Him a lunatic; His enemies insinuated that He was the chosen emissary of the chief of devils. But the appreciative declared that He was one of Israel's true prophets. It was high praise: in their judgment He came up to the best in the nation's great past. But Jesus recalled the fate of the prophets. Was His to be a career ending like Elijah's in triumph or like Jeremiah's in a series of indignities? A prophet—was He not more than that in His own consciousness of His mission? And His mind is brooding over what is in immediate prospect for Him.

So, brushing aside the opinions of a sympathetic public, He asks His closest friends to tell Him frankly how they rate Him. Peter breaks silence with the acknowledgment that they find in Him the Son of God, the Messiah, who sums up Israel's hopes and ushers in the Reign of God. We can scarcely overestimate the satisfaction it must have given Jesus to hear from the lips of one who knew Him intimately the echo of His own thought of Himself. At last He is understood. But at once would occur the haunting suggestion, Do they understand? Can they know what is in My mind?

He faces afresh His own view of His career. How He had reached it we shall never fully know. He has thought of the treatment accorded God's messengers through the centuries: "The blood of all the prophets which was shed from the foundation of the world." His mind has been vividly impressed

with the recent fate of John the Baptist. His
poetic insight into the ways of nature discloses harvests produced from seed which dies
in lonely darkness and man born of woman in
travail. He recalls the outcome of the career
of that mysterious Servant of the Lord in
the prophet's haunting message, wounded for
others' transgressions and bruised for their
iniquities, and by His death making many
righteous. However He came by His views,
He startled these friends by announcing:
"The Son of man must suffer and be killed."
No doubt details have been added by subsequent interpreters, but He said enough to
shock these men and bring Peter's protest:
"This shall never be unto Thee." Once more
Jesus finds Himself at grips with other ideals
of His work. Here are His staunchest friends,
men like Himself prepared to stake their lives
for the hope of Israel, and they cannot see
this part of His programme. May they not
be right? Their opinions must surely have
strained Him as heavily as the opinions of the
best folk of the time which He had faced in
His solitary hours in the wilderness. "Get

thee behind me, Satan: thy thoughts **are** man's, not God's."

So He is driven back again to face God's thought for Him. What we call the Transfiguration is the experience, confusedly reported by dazed disciples, through which He and they passed in that critical moment. Luke tells us Jesus was praying—consciously seeking His Father's purpose for Him. Jesus Himself, according to our first evangelist, calls the experience "a vision." If we are right in thinking that it was the fate of the prophets of the olden time that was uppermost in His mind, we can see how the careers of Moses and Elijah would claim His attention. Both had mysteriously glorious exits from our earth. Would His be like theirs? Or would it be a tragic death? Behind that scene on the mountain is another spiritual struggle, in which He confronts the outcome of His career and determines His immediate course. In that experience He rises out of the society of His most devoted companions into the loftier fellowship of the saints of old, and for a moment His companions realize it. He emerges resolved to go to the capital. He is open-eyed to the probable result: Jerusalem killed the prophets and stoned them that were sent unto her. How far He went in thinking through what His death might achieve, we may not be able to say. But He was plainly counting the cost, and was prepared to pay it even with His blood.

When Montaigne was asked to become mayor of Bordeaux, he replied with a significant reservation: "I am willing to take the city's affairs on my hands, but not on my heart or my liver." His public services must not tax his health or strain his constitution. The resolve to attempt Jerusalem meant for Jesus the risking of His life, and He willingly staked it. When one thinks what He was leaving behind, one is confident that He believed that His death would be gain for His cause. He might have gone on for years in Galilee most helpfully. Think of the teaching He might have done, of the relief He might have given sufferers, of the friendship with which He might have enriched hundreds! Life meant more to Him than to others. He

[64]

would not hazard it lightly. "Greater love hath no man than this that a man lay down his life." Surely He must have persuaded Himself that His death would not damage His cause.

How did He forefancy its result? We may look at three explanations which He is said to have made of it, explanations which go back to our earliest narratives about him. Critics are skeptical of interpretations which may reflect the subsequent thought of the Church, but it is plain that Jesus must have had reasons for hazarding Himself in that venture at Jerusalem, and these are the reasons to which He alludes in our most trustworthy sources.

He spoke of His death as a baptism, "The baptism that I am baptized with." Another evangelist has a similar saying: "I have a baptism to be baptized with, and how am I straitened till it be accomplished." It is a word which had been given a special meaning to that generation by the work of John, and a word which recalled for Jesus an outstanding spiritual experience of His own. It stood for a symbolic rite which equipped those who underwent it for God's kingdom. Death—a death so terrible that He shudders as He thinks of it—will be His anointing to bring in the Reign of God. From this baptism of blood He will come with power to fulfil His God-assigned task. What faith to see in this ordeal an equipment for His Messiahship! Through an engulfing sea of pain and death He will emerge baptized,

> . . . with new acquist
> Of true experience from this great event.

Again, when His disciples are wrangling among themselves over questions of rank, He suddenly mentions His death: "The Son of Man came not to be ministered unto but to minister, and to give His life a ransom for many." It is difficult not to hear in this saying echoes of the Suffering Servant portrayed by the prophet. His death will be of a piece with His life—a service. It will accomplish a great emancipation. It will inaugurate the new era of freedom, in which the chiefest is servant of all. To press the metaphor and ask to whom Jesus thought the ransom was paid is to abuse His figurative language. He is confident that His vicarious Self-offering will achieve that new day of liberty for self-bound men of which prophets had spoken and which He had proclaimed in His own teaching.

The third expression occurs in the Upper Room, where as He hands the cup to His disciples, He speaks of it as "My blood of the covenant, which is poured out for many." Old Testament hopes are in His mind. His sacrifice will establish that intimate fellowship with God in which men's inmost feelings and motives shall accord with His will. He is so sure of it that this meal where a few friends eat and drink with Him becomes to Him a foretaste of the glad Messianic age, and He speaks of drinking the wine new with them in His Father's kingdom.

These sayings lift a veil and let us see what was in Jesus' mind. Scholars may question this or that phrase, but without the interpretation which such sayings furnish, we are at a loss to know why He abandoned His fruitful ministry in Galilee and resolved to imperil

Himself at the capital. Why should He give up a useful career, blessed of God, and bring on a conflict, almost inevitably fatal, at Jerusalem? He must have become convinced that His death, even more effectively than a continuation of His work of teaching and healing and friendship, would set up His Father's reign over His children and bring them abundant life. He is not blind to the danger before Him; He sees a violent death awaiting Him. By the light of the loftiest Divine ideal in the religious heritage of His people, He explains the result. His journey to the capital is a deliberate act of Self-offering.

With this interpretation of His mind the manner of His entry into Jerusalem becomes explicable. Jesus usually shunned publicity and avoided the spectacular. The reported ride into the capital is so out of character that its historicity has been challenged. But if we have at all correctly sensed His mind, it is in keeping with His purpose. He is offering Himself publicly to the nation. He is using another prophetic picture, a picture which both in the inclusiveness of its promised re-

sults and in the character of its central figure
accords with the description of the Servant
of the Lord in the book of Isaiah.

Here comes your King
triumphant and victorious
riding humbly on an ass,
on the foal of an ass!
He banishes all chariots from Ephraim,
war-horses from Jerusalem,
and battle-bows;
His words make peace for nations,
His sway extends from sea to sea,
from the Euphrates to the ends of the earth.

He who thought in pictures will enact this picture for the city whose citizens are familiar
with the regal religious tradition. Some have
thought that the public entry into Jerusalem
was forced upon Him by His enthusiastic followers; but our narratives represent Him as
planning it and arranging its details. It is an
acted parable into which He puts His ideal of
God's Representative, and offers Himself to
the nation.

He is challenging attention. Will the leaders accept Him and receive that which He

brings them? He can hardly have expected
it. He had seen enough of the religious authorities to know that this would have no appeal for them. The publicity of His entrance
into the capital courted death.

Further, once in the city, He makes for the
Temple. He will give the leaders of the
Church no chance to ignore Him. There He
presumes to cleanse the court of money-
changers. His is no uncontrolled nature overcome by sudden impulse; He acts deliberately.
He knows that He is bringing on Himself the
ill-will of the powerful who direct the affairs of the national Church. He is certainly
not dragged reluctantly into open conflict
with the leaders. He makes it impossible for
them to overlook Him. The fourth evangelist is not overstating the plain facts of the
story when he reports Christ as saying: "I
lay down my life of Myself."

But what are Jesus' feelings as He forces
the issue? Let us think again of Him who
had placed Himself beside penitent sinners in
the Jordan. He reaches the holy city for
which, like every devout Jew, He felt a pa-

triot's love. It is cold to Him, God's Representative. With an assurance akin to that of the great prophet's He is confident of its doom. "O Jerusalem, Jerusalem!" is His heart-broken cry. His feelings are torn: on the one hand His conscience is in accord with God's judgment on an unresponsive people; on the other hand His heart grieves over countless little ones blindly fated to destruction. In 1877 Richard Green, the historian of the English people, distressed by the public policy of the nation, wrote in a letter:

I love England dearly. But I love her too well to wish her triumphant if she fights against human right and human freedom. Pitt longed for her defeat in America, but it killed him when it came. I can understand that double feeling now.

And it is a similar "double feeling" which we see in Jesus. He belongs to the unresponsive nation and is involved in its guilt and weeps over its approaching doom. He is God's Representative and must bring on the crisis in order that the kingdom may come.

Yes, by forcing the issue He makes more sure of His own death, and that fills up the measure of His loved people's iniquity. If a "double feeling" in an English statesman's heart killed him, we gain some insight into a similar struggle in the anguished soul of Christ.

We follow Him to Gethsemane. In the Upper Room He has said with assurance: "The Son of man goeth even as it is written of Him." But in the garden He is pleading for some other issue. Has He changed His purpose? We may explain His prayer by the natural shrinking from an appalling ordeal when it actually arrives, however clearly it has been anticipated. Men prepare themselves for a loved one's death, and even admit that they think it is for the best, but when the hour of parting comes their affection cannot help pleading that the dear life be spared to them. And the struggle in Gethsemane means more than this. An acute New Testament interpreter sees in it a battle with doubt: "He suffered, being tempted."

What were the doubts which haunted Jesus

in Gethsemane and on to the very moment of His losing consciousness in death?

One surely must have been doubt of the wisdom of the course He had taken in bringing on this clash and leading His little company of followers into it. He could feel that His friends were baffled by Him and could not grasp what He was doing. Perhaps He already felt them slipping from Him, and so chose the most responsive three to go into the garden. If even His closest intimates did not understand Him would His death advance the cause He had at heart? Would it not damage it irreparably? Would He not lose the loyal few and send His cherished purpose into oblivion?

We have moments of insight when we feel sure that we see our way—a way which we dare to affirm is God's way for us; but the next morning are we so serenely confident? And when our course involves others who trust our leadership, and when a cause hangs on our decision, into what an abyss doubt can fling a man!

In 1837 Mazzini found himself in London,

in "the hell of exile" as he calls it, reduced
to pawning his clothes for food, and tormented by uncertainty whether he had done
rightly in leading others to sacrifice their for-
tunes and their lives for a united Italy. He
writes:

I felt myself a criminal. The forms of
those shot at Alessandria and Chambéry rose
up before me like the phantoms of a crime
and its unavailing remorse. I could not recall them to life. How many mothers I had
caused to weep! How many more must learn
to weep, should I persist in the attempt to
rouse the youth of Italy to noble action, to
awaken in them the yearning for a common
country! And if that country were indeed an
illusion!

There are few more depressing hours than
those in which an earnest man is forced to
ask himself whether he is not mistaken. The
more intensely he cares for his cause, the
more terrible is the thought that he may be
jeopardizing it by going about it in the wrong
way. If he is staking his all upon it, what
if he be throwing away his life? Worse yet,

if he is followed trustfully by others, there is no agony of mind more torturing than the misgiving that he is subjecting them to danger for nothing. "He suffered, being tempted."

Again He must have been tempted to question the salvability of the men for whom He was laying down His life. He had never cherished illusions as to the responsiveness of everyone to the highest appeals. The first parable on His lips is that in which He pictures His message falling on four kinds of soil, and only one out of the four proves productive. He faced man's ignorance: "If thou hadst known," He wept over Jerusalem. What reason had He to suppose she would ever know? If she had been blind to His teaching, would her eyes be opened to One who hung a felon on a gibbet? "They know not what they do," He was to pray of His executioners. But why should He fancy that they would wake to what they had done? He had been obliged to say to the men whom He had taught repeatedly: "Do ye not yet understand?" As He looked at His sleeping disciples, and again as He confronted the

Sanhedrin, Pontius Pilate, Herod, the crowd in the judgment-hall, the soldiers in the guard-room, the staring eyes of hundreds at the place of execution, must not His heart have sunk within Him? Would they or any-one else ever have the faintest inkling of what He was doing for them? He was lay-ing down His life, "a ransom for many"; but were there many big enough to appreciate such self-offering? Indeed were there any? One might die for men, if one were sure that one's death would alter them. But would it? When the crowd shouted "Not this Man, but Barabbas," what doubts as to the result of His death must have come to the mind of Jesus? "He suffered, being tempted."

And at the last He seems to have doubted the faithfulness of God. He was staking everything on that. The figure of the vicari-ously suffering Servant of mankind had mas-tered His conscience because it had seemed to Him what God is—One who bears His children's sins with and for them, and thus redeems them. But that was not the God most men believed in then, any more than it is the God in whom the majority believe to-day. Jesus saw traces of such a God in nature —in seeds which die in solitary darkness and bring into being the fields of grain which feed a world. He saw such a God more clearly in human nature at its best—in shepherds who risk their lives for their sheep, in mothers who forget the anguish of child-birth for joy that a man is born into the world, in prophets and righteous men who pour out their blood that fellow-countrymen may be inspired to justice and liberty and faith. But these were only occasional glimpses. To Him as to our-selves nature appeared morally indifferent: its sun shone on evil and good, its rains fell on just and unjust. The tower of Siloam had fallen on men no worse than their neighbors. There are

> Fallings from us, vanishings
> Blank misgivings of the creature,

what William James calls "The sick shudder of the frustrated religious demand." Suppose God were to let His offered life go for nought? Is not that the haggard misgiving that dogged Him to the very last, and wrung from Him the cry of dereliction: "My God, My God, why hast Thou forsaken Me?" "He suffered, being tempted."

And not only did Jesus battle with doubt, but He struggled with an overwhelming moral confusion. Is He justified in forcing the leaders of the nation on to a supreme crime which will have appalling consequences? The "double feeling" may serve to render vivid to us the acuteness of His spiritual conflict. We cannot account for His recoil from the cross save as we remember His sense of kinship with those who were reddening their hands with the blood of the Representative of their God, and bringing judgment upon their and His people. He is the conscience of His less conscientious brothers. He realizes, as they cannot, the enormity of what they are doing and its dire sequel in this moral universe. The utter and hideous ungodlikeness of men was expressed for Him in those who would have none of Him, and cried "Away with Him! Crucify Him!" He saw doom about to break: "Daughters of Jerusalem, weep not for Me, but weep for yourselves and for your children." And He was hastening that disaster in the very effort to emancipate His brethren and cause the day of light and love to dawn. These folk, blind to their peace, were His people. He was stedfast to His Father's purpose, but might not there be an alternative which had not been disclosed to Him? The situation is too terrible. "Abba, all things are possible unto Thee; remove this cup from Me: howbeit not what I will, but what Thou wilt."

And when that struggle in the garden passes and He goes to His ordeal, another struggle is to be undergone upon the cross itself. His keen social conscience, which made His own the guilt of all who were slaying Him, and His acute sympathy with them in their blindness and estrangement from God, brought Him into the midnight of forsakenness. "I felt," writes John Woolman, the Quaker, "the depth and extent of the misery of my fellow creatures, separated from the Divine harmony, and it was greater than I could bear, and I was crushed down under it." From the lowest depth which any of His followers have touched we may venture to look down further still into the abyss in which Jesus felt Himself bereft of God.

But with chance after chance to escape— for even from Gethsemane Jesus might have slipped off in the darkness and fled the city— He still continued to face death as God's purpose for Him. Battling with doubts and tormented with moral perplexities, He hazarded everything on this offering of Himself in sacrifice. It is the crowning instance of faith. He has His own interpretation of the ultimate Mystery of the universe, His own intuition of God. He is not slavishly following an ideal of the Servant of the Lord in the inherited religion of His people. If that ideal is in His mind, it grips and holds Him because it recurs persistently as the mind of the God in whom He cannot but believe. It is His Father's will that He should drain this cup of bitter pain and accursed death. And by faith He endures the cross.

There is a mystery here which we cannot penetrate. Why is vicarious suffering necessary? Life is full of instances of it, but it still remains dark to our understandings. Why must One take on His conscience the sins of countless others and offer Himself in sacrifice? Jesus supplies no answer. Very likely He had none. Men of religious insight in various faiths had discovered this strange principle in life that the innocent suffer with and for the guilty, and that the voluntary self-offering of the good for the evil reconciles the community with God and works social right-eousness. It is a fact to be recognized, however incapable we may be of rationalizing it. The finest spirits in Israel were clearly aware of it. In the first public act of His ministry Jesus identified Himself with His sinful people, and in His last He let Himself be hanged, condemned by Church and State. Why must such things be? To Jesus this was not some dark decree of fate, but His Father's will, and His Father is good.

Was Jesus' faith in God correct? Is there in and over this bewildering scheme of things One who cares and loves? One who wills men's deliverance from evil? One whose fittest representative is He whose conscience accepts as His obligation the ill-doing of all and offers Himself to compass their redemption? Is God Self-giving?

Jesus' faith is widely doubted, but wistfully doubted. At the commencement at Harvard University a few years ago a poet said:

Our faiths have fallen from us and left us
    bare;
The dream, fantastic and compassionate,
That like a veil of love and glory hung
Between us and the bitterness of things,
Is lifted, and the universe has grown
Vaster and much more lonely. Nor shall
    Thought—
Crying into the dark, and listening, listen-
    ing—
Find any answer to her prayer: the night
Is soundless, and the starry mouths are
    sealed.

To wistful folk feeling like that there is nothing so helpful as Christ on the cross. He is Comrade of their woesome desertion. They may be disposed to say to Him, as Carlyle is alleged to have remarked once, when he was passing a wayside crucifix in Brittany: "Poor Chap! your day is done." But they feel that He shares their plight beneath an impassive sky. The Best our earth has known, the most conscientious, met the slings and arrows of outrageous fortune and was left to die while all things moved in their unheeding course.

Jesus on the cross is the challenge to the universe. If He goes down to defeat, if He is forsaken, then the heavens are empty, and the whole scheme of things heartless, godless. Man fights "a lone fight against a vast indifference."

But the crucifixion is not the final scene in our gospels, and, apart from the gospels, on the pages of the world's history, it is not an event without a sequel. His enemies felt that they had given Him and His cause a quietus. They supposed that He might survive somewhere, but He was banished from their earth, and would never again disturb Jerusalem. Whatever interpretations may be put on the details of the narratives of the resurrection, and however we may explain the occurrence itself, something momentous took place. That is indisputable. The universe did not remain inactive and indifferent. A company of world-conquering folk, imbued with Christ's Spirit, was born. The Church of Christ became alive with power. In this embodiment, and beyond the confines of the fellowship of those who know themselves members of the Body of Christ, His Spirit has been working mightily even until now. Jesus' faith in God has been vindicated. His reading of the ultimate mystery has been proved correct by the redemptive power given Him age after age. In and over the world is One akin to Him in heart and conscience, responsive to His vicarious Self-offering.

Not many of the small radio sets in people's homes can as yet pick up directly sounds which come across the Atlantic; but some powerful central station receives and relays them. Then the small radio sets get them. Men's minds are often blank with bewilderment in this baffling world; our spirits listen vainly, encompassed apparently by a silent void. Jesus' soul was sensitive and attuned to the Most Highest: His believing intuitions have been verified. A faithful Father received into His hands this Son and His cause, and Jesus' sacrifice of Himself for many has been the birth-pangs of a new creation. Enduring the cross He has become the Pioneer and Perfection of faith, and the Redeemer of men.

HOW SHALL WE INTERPRET THE CROSS?

CHAPTER III

WE have sought to give reality to the exposition of the cross by approaching the subject with two straight-forward questions of history:—How came the Best of men to be executed? and Why did Jesus deliberately go to His death? We must now attempt to gather up some of the items in our message of Christ crucified. An apostle called it "the wisdom of God," suggesting that it gives us a clue by which to interpret our world and ourselves and God. How, then, shall we use it as "wisdom"?

We must take the evils from which we would deliver men and look at them in their connection with this supreme tragedy. The religious word for wickedness is sin, and for us Christians sin is disharmony with the purpose of God revealed in Christ. Sin's nature is made plain in that dying Figure on the gibbet. Sin is murderous to all we most admire. If Jesus be for us the Representative of God, sin is deicidal. Golgotha reminds us that ruinous forces reside in and dominate our world, that in men's spirits are suicidal tendencies which drive them to kill the God-like in themselves. According to one reading of a sentence in the Epistle to the Hebrews, it was this self-destructive force in men which caused Christ His agony: "Consider Him that hath endured such gainsaying of sinners *against themselves*." We live surrounded by tragedy. The fateful character of the struggle between love and selfishness, between wisdom and folly, between God and whatever thwarts His will, is made plain to us in the tortured Sufferer.

In our preaching we must take specific sins and show men their connection with the cross. Here is the common habit of passing on our opinions about other people—gossip. What is Calvary but the result of an accumulation of such opinions—rumors carried to Jerusalem, judgments formed without investigation, impressions taken at second-hand and let harden into prejudices so that a subsequent first-hand impression is discolored and distorted. When one thinks of the loose talk about people, which forms the staple of conversation in many circles, is not George Meredith correct when he calls gossip "a beast of prey that does not wait for the death of the creature it devours"?

Here is industrial strife allowed to develop to such a crisis that strikers or guards are killed, or here are industrial maladjustments suffered to produce situations where the unemployed starve or shoot themselves in desperation. Is not the collective heartlessness and thoughtlessness behind these social murders of a piece with the motives which sent Jesus to Golgotha?

Here is unchastity, lightly spoken of to-day as the expression of sex, and widely heralded as socially harmless and even beneficial for the individual, provided it be indulged in with hygienic safeguards and under circumstances which prevent the procreation of children. Viewed in the light of the cross, is not such temporary physical relationship with another human being akin to that contempt for personality which spoke of the death of Jesus as expedient?

Here is war. A British sergeant on the Somme has said that through those long months when the two battle-lines kept up their continuous exchange of shells, he could not get away from the feeling that Christ was out between the lines and that the shot passed through His body. Certainly war between fellow-Christians pierces and tears the Body of Christ, which is the Church. And the systematized butchery of fellow-men re-enacts Calvary.

Here are racial prejudices—the feeling of so-called Christians that Jews are inherently their social inferiors whom in various ways they may ostracize, or the feeling of white folk that Negroes are a race to be permanently kept in a subordinate position as hewers of wood and drawers of water and denied the full opportunities for development which the white race enjoys. Is not this attitude at one with the scourging and crucifixion meted to a provincial from which a Roman citizen was immune?

We bring home to men's consciences the deadly fatality of their customary ways and their habitual assumptions when we link them with the crucifixion of the Son of God. Newman well said: "Our great security against sin lies in being shocked at it." The Spanish author, Miguel de Unamuno, has entitled a striking book "The Tragic Sense of Life in Men and in Peoples." Without this tragic sense there can be little religion worthy the name. The cross is the supreme tragedy with which the seemingly trifling or readily condoned sins must be connected by the preacher of the Gospel. He will help men to achieve the prayer by which Unamuno concludes his book: "May God deny you peace, but give you glory."

And we can preach Christ as sharing with us fully this tragedy. Despite the advances of man's intelligence, mystery does not disappear from the universe, nor from every man's experience of life and pain and death. The problem of suffering and the problem of evil remain insoluble. Every pastor stands again and again beside men and women whose hearts wrung with anguish ask, Why? Usually there is no satisfactory answer.

Thoughtful spirits pass through seasons when the sum of human misery and wrong becomes more than they can bear. Human life is often sordid, cruel, bestial. Ruskin once wrote of it as "a river of blood which can but sweep me down in the midst of its black clots helpless." Calvary is the evidence that Christ was engulfed in this very stream, and that means everything to those in like case. Dora Greenwell tells us:

The mystery of the cross did not, it is true, explain any one of the enigmas connected with our mortal existence and destiny, but it linked itself in my spirit with them all. It was itself an enigma flung down by God alongside the sorrowful problem of human life, the confession of Omnipotence itself to some stern reality of misery and wrong.

Jesus tasted helplessness: "He was crucified through weakness." He knew our bewilderment: "My God, why?" He experienced the confusion of a mind which darts off in every direction seeking an alternative, and is hurled back baffled: "If it be possible."

[94]

He stood aghast before an ordeal which staggered Him: "Let this cup pass away from Me." He faced the inevitable—the grim thing that must be: "If this cup cannot pass from Me except I drink it." He underwent the last loneliness—separation from all He loved and the feeling of desertion by God. No one can plumb the depths of His suffering.

Over the abyss
Of God's capacity for woe He stayed
One hesitating hour; what gulf was this?
Forsaken He went down, and was afraid.

We have no explanations to offer perplexed souls in many of the circumstances which raise the insistent, Why? But we have a Figure to set before them, a Fellow-sufferer, who dies with an unanswered question on His lips, yet dies placing Himself in a Father's hands. That Figure throughout the Christian centuries has riveted the attention of men in their most tragic experiences. They look at Him and find sympathy, and through Him they regain faith. In the Louvre there is a painting of Christ on the cross by Francia with a kneeling figure shrouded in darkness at its foot, looking up at the inscription *Et maiora sustinuit Ipse*—And greater pains than thine has He endured. A novelist of the last generation brings one of her characters to the same place, and comments:

The only thought that seemed to soothe the torture of imagination was the thought stamped on her brain tissue by the long inheritance of centuries—the thought of Christ on Calvary. "My God, My God, why hast Thou forsaken Me?" The words repeated themselves again and again. She did not pray in words. But her agony crept to the foot of what has become, through the action and interaction of two thousand years, the typical and representative agony of the world, and, clinging there, made wild appeal, like the generations before her, to a God in whose hand lie the creatures of His will.

To bewildered folk, caught in life's confusions, it is steadying and comforting to be shown the Crucified. They recognize Him at once as Comrade of their perplexity. The darkness which enveloped Him at Golgotha is a symbol of their plight. And His commitment of Himself to a God, who commanded His confidence even when He puzzled Him, seems the Gospel they need. The writer to the Hebrews had insight when he saw that Jesus was perfected as the Helper of men "by the things which He experienced." T. E. Lawrence, perhaps the most picturesque and certainly one of the sadly disillusioned commanders in the Great War, tells us that the Arabs taught him, "that no man could be their leader except he ate the ranks' food, wore their clothes, lived level with them, and yet appeared better in himself." How apt a commentary on the description of Christ as "tempted in all points like as we are, yet without sin," and thus fitted to be the Captain leading us into the life with God.

Again we can preach Christ as bearing our sins. We must be careful to draw no sharp distinction in this between what He did in His life and in His death; in both He encounters the force of evil and offers Himself to deliver men from its thraldom. On the cross He bore the sins of His time and society

in the sense of being the Victim of their im-
placable hostility. And He bore them on His
conscience when He identified Himself with
sinners and voluntarily gave His life an
emancipation for many. These sins are the
corporate sins of humanity. Jesus did not
consciously assume the iniquity of an ancient
Egyptian under the Pharaohs who grafted
in a contract on the pyramids, or the wickedness of a white-slaver who in 1931 inveigles
a girl to a life of shame. He bore the collective sins of the community of His day. Modern thinkers stress the solidarity of our race
throughout its generations. We are members
one of another by ties which run not only
laterally to our contemporaries but also line-
ally, linking the centuries by social heredity.
The cross is a family catastrophe, in which
the actors are our kinsmen, and the blood of
the Victim stains us as sharers in our brothers'
crime. Evil is one vast corporate force
throughout the ages. The selfish impulse, the
callous indifference, the suspicion, the conceit,
in you and me are identical in principle with
that sinister combination of motives which

drove the nails through Christ's hands and feet. The spark of electricity which meets the touch of one's hand on a metal knob of a winter's morning is one with the bolt of lightning which wrecks a house. Men of awakened conscience, faced with Christ on the cross, feel themselves involved in that tragedy.

And Jesus bears sin in the sense of bearing it away. His death on Calvary is the most potent reinforcement of righteousness in human history, a reinforcement which continues with unabated power age after age. George Tyrrell, the Roman Catholic Modernist, in his combat with ecclesiastical tyranny and ignorance, writes: ₽ 7864

Again and again I have been tempted to give up the struggle, but always the figure of that Strange Man hanging on the cross sends me back to my task again.

An African convert in Bechuanaland, in a testimony meeting, used the striking phrase: "The cross of Christ condemns me to be a saint."

This power of Christ's cross to redeem

from evil and impel to goodness is due to the
fact that our present sins become identified
with the evils which crucified Him and seem
to re-enact Golgotha for Him. John Mase-
field has put it vividly when he makes the
Quakeress in his poem say to the besotted
drunkard, Saul Kane:*

> When next you drink
> Do me the gentleness to think
> That every drop of drink accursed
> Makes Christ within you die of thirst,
> That every dirty word you say
> Is one more flint upon His way,
> Another thorn around His head,
> Another mock by where He tread,
> Another nail, another cross.
> All that you are is that Christ's loss.

This portrayal of his life as a continuation
of Calvary is Saul Kane's deliverance:

> The bolted door had broken in,
> I knew that I had done with sin.
> I knew that Christ had given me birth
> To brother all the souls on earth.
> And every bird and every beast
> Should share the crumbs broke at the feast.

*By permission of The Macmillan Company, publishers.

The intuitions of our poets have preserved the essential meaning of the cross when many theologians were missing it. Christ the Sin-bearer is pre-eminently Christ the Saviour. We must make plain that, by no artificial legal transaction, but by the solidarity of our sin with the factors which crucified Him, what we are to-day in our selfishness is "that Christ's loss."

In bearing sin for us there is a sense in which we speak of Christ as our substitute. He in His life and on the cross does some-thing for us which we, thanks to Him, are relieved from doing. Those of us who spend our holidays in the mountains know our in-debtedness to trail-makers, who blazed paths through the forest and set up cairns on the slopes of the summits above the timber line. They have undergone for us the uncertainty and toil of discovering the route which avoids an impassable crevasse, which takes us around some subordinate peak, which carries us up a favoring ridge with fine outlook, which skirts a precipitate side and sets us on an open approach to the top. We need not repeat their experiments nor taste their sense of being baffled. They reached the summit and have marked for us a sure way. We profit by their finished task in the well-indicated trail. What they did, they did for many.

But this does not mean that their work relieves us of effort. We must climb the path they have marked and cover every step of the distance to the peak in order to enjoy the prospect.

In taking on His conscience the sin of the world and in letting men slay Him, our Lord suffered the Righteous for the unrighteous. He offered this sacrifice of Himself once for all. He discovered the path to oneness with God—the path of trust and devotion, the path of love which beareth, believeth, hopeth, endureth all and never faileth. He blazed that trail with His blood. Or (to employ a New Testament metaphor) He opened a new and living way. The trail once found and marked, the way once opened, remains for all time. None can repeat the vicarious sacrifice of Him who gave Himself to discover the route, to be the Way. Forever all who attain like oneness with God must come unto the Father through Him. And all will be grateful to Him "the Pioneer and Perfection of faith," "the Author of eternal salvation."

But He is Saviour only to those who obey Him. The path of trust and devotion must be trod by those who wish to share His life with God. The trail of vicarious love is to be taken and pursued until we, too, bear the sins of men and offer ourselves in service for their redemption. "He laid down His life for us, and we ought also to lay down our lives for the brethren." Christ is both substitute and exemplar. Every Christian has his part in making up "the deficit" (to quote St. Paul's metaphor) in Christ's sufferings for His Body's sake, which is the Church.

This is "the wisdom of God" in delivering His children through Christ crucified from their sins and making them partners in the salvation of the world. But it is not a wisdom confined to the Christian Gospel. It would be strange if so profound a human need should not have found a Divine response through other faiths. In Buddhism, for example, one sees men reaching out to the many loved mythical heroes, and praising them for their rescues of their unworthy devotees. The mediæval Tamil Manikkar Vachakar in a hymn to Shiva, sings:

Thou mad'st me Thine, didst fiery poison eat,
That I might eat with Thee the food of
    heaven,
I meanest one, O thou Compassionate.

It does not derogate from the worth of Christ that men have known other saviours who awakened their loyalty. He does not suffer from comparison with these divinities; rather He towers above them in His ethical supremacy; and the craving which they have roused, and in part satisfied, He lays hold on and satisfies completely. The religious experience of these non-Christian faiths is not to be depreciated. Their saints have been to some extent kinsmen in spirit of Jesus and have prepared the way for His Gospel.

Again it is by inducing men to see themselves in the light of the cross that we bring them God's estimate of their value. We never are more appalled by ourselves than when we think of our complicity in Calvary. We shudder at ourselves, and abhor ourselves; but the cross does not give us, as one of our hymns claims, a sense of our own "worthlessness." Emily Dickinson in a letter comments caustically on a sermon to which she had been listening.

Presume if I met with my deserts I should receive nothing. Was informed to that effect to-day by a dear Pastor. What a privilege it is to be so insignificant! Thought of intimating that the Atonement was not needed for such atoms.

Has aught given men a nobler appreciation of their worth than this that the Son of God died for them? They may have known themselves pariahs or slaves in the eyes of the world; but Christ has deemed them worth dying for. The French scholar, Muretus, a Protestant exile from Toulouse in the seventeenth century, fell seriously ill in Lombardy, and was taken to a pauper hospital, where he overheard the physicians who were consulting about him say in Latin, not thinking that the pauper could understand that tongue of the learned: *"Faciamus experimentum in anima vili"* ("Let us try an experiment with this worthless creature"). And from his bed the sick scholar startled them by murmuring: *"Vilem animam appellas pro qua Christus non dedignatus est mori?"* ("Will you call worthless one for whom Christ did not disdain to die?")

The cross abides a challenge to belittling views of one's self. To every man come times when he is oppressed with his own Liliputian insignificance—one among such swarming myriads of his kind, an ephemeral being whose span of life is a mere wink in the duration of our ancient planet, a dweller upon one of the meaner bodies in a system of innumerable stars, a walking chemical laboratory driven by instincts of hunger and sex. But if one believes himself redeemed by the blood of Christ, he cannot hold himself cheap.

It may be said that it is inflated egotism which interprets the cross so personally. Christ's life was laid down for His community and through it for the race. It is an exaggeration to see in it a special love for an individual. But from the days of St. Paul men have spoken of it as though there were a direct connection between Christ crucified and themselves: "who loved me and gave Himself up for me." If one stands beside the ocean on a moonlight night, he sees a straight path of silver from the moon to his own feet. There is no escaping it. If he moves miles in either direction, the beam of light continues to lie directly between him and the moon. There is something in the action of light and in the structure of his eyes which renders this inescapable. Every man who looks wistfully towards the cross finds a similar direct nexus between the Crucified and himself. As there is a solidarity which links man's sin to-day with the wickedness of those who slew Christ, so there is a ray of love which appears to come straight to him from the heart of the Saviour. He cannot get away from it. Christ's sacrifice has a personal meaning for him; and in that love he knows his own incalculable worth to God.

This is not to exalt a man in egotism. Any thoughtful person realizes that every other pair of eyes sees the moon sending its ribbon of silvery light as directly to them. A Christian thinks of every man's life as shined upon by the cross. The crank and the weakling and the good-for-nothing are brothers for whose sake Christ died.

There are many tendencies in our time which lead us to think lightly of human beings. What of the thousands of mental defectives, of the economically unemployable, of backward races, of chronic criminals, whom we lump in statistical tables. The evolutionary outlook on life tempts us to class the socially unfit with the physically or mentally unfit in their environments among lower forms which have been eliminated. But the rubbish heap to which society is disposed to consign its useless or dangerous members is the spot to which Christ turns with keenest interest. One cannot forget prostitutes and tax-farmers, the little ones whom the community rated of no account, the bandit who hung beside Him at Golgotha. He was always after "the lost."

His cross has put a new valuation on human-ity's refuse. The socially unfit are not to be eliminated but redeemed, and no price is too costly to lavish on their redemption. "I hungered for hell," said old General Booth in a revealing moment which discloses his Chris-tian interest in the offscourings of mankind. The poorest specimen the race can show is worth the outlay of the life of the Son of God. All cheapening views of human beings —hands to be bought in the labor market, natives to be exploited where white toilers would be dear, criminals to be dealt with as warnings to the lawless—are repugnant to those who believe in Christ crucified for sin-ners.

Again it is in our preaching of the cross that we have our fullest opportunity to set forth the Christian conception of God. The death of Jesus is to Christians the most re-vealing event in history. In the Crucified God has become frankest and disclosed His inmost heart.

This is a point which requires careful treatment. The revolt from various theories of the Atonement has been due to their unchristian views of God. A Father who had to be reconciled to His children, whose wrath had to be appeased or whose forgiveness could be purchased, is not the Father of Jesus Christ—the God in whom He believed and whose character He revealed in His teaching and whose nature was embodied in Himself. William Blake is alleged to have said of the current preaching of the cross in his day: "First God the Father fetches us a clout on the head, then Christ brings us balm for our wounds." Even in some recent restatements of the doctrine, by men apparently sympathetic with modern thinking, God is depersonalized into a principle of righteousness or loses His heart in His holiness. But this is not only to be false to the God in whom Jesus believed; it is to do less than justice to the God of historic theology. John Calvin wrote: "God the Father doth with His love precede and go before our reconciliation in Christ; yea, because He first loves us, therefore He afterwards doth reconcile us unto Himself."*

*"Institutes," book II, chapter XVI, 3.

We must begin with our fundamental Christian conviction that God is known in Jesus: "He that hath seen Me hath seen the Father." The first interpreters of the cross, and Jesus Himself, thought of the vicarious sin-bearer as the Servant of the Lord. It was His Father's will that He should offer Himself, and the Father's will is the Father's very essence. Vicarious suffering is grounded in the nature of God. His Servant represents and reveals Him. There is a painting in the National Gallery in London in which one sees Christ on the cross against a black background. Darkness wraps Him in loneliness. He, and He only, loves enough to suffer and die. The universe is uncaring. But if one looks intently there emerges from the blackness the dim outline of another crucified Sufferer—the Father sharing Golgotha with His Son.

Nor did the Divine sacrifice begin at Calvary. From the foundation of the world life has been born of pain and death, and self-giving for others has been part of the constitution of the race of living creatures.

Mystic writers have connected the agony outside the wall of Jerusalem with the travail of
the creation. A modern poet writes:

All living creatures' pain,
The suffering of the lowliest thing that creeps
Or flies a moment ere it sinks and sleeps
Are too Redemption's tears and not in vain—
For nothing idly weeps.
Earth is through these fulfilling that it must
As in Christ's own eternal Passion chain,
And flowering from the dust.

The struggle for the existence of others is as
inherent in the cosmic process as the effort to
maintain one's own existence, and the law of
self-sacrifice is as patent as the law of self-
preservation.

And apart from these links between Calvary
and the fabric of life itself, the God in whom
Jesus believed had shared the experiences of
His children, afflicted in all their affliction,
vexed and grieved and burdened by their
wrong-doing, and patiently giving Himself
to bring them to a better mind. A modern Jew
has given vivid expression to this ancient
Hebrew thought of God. Mr. Zangwill, in

"The Cockpit," makes the Queen scornfully comment on the New Testament phrase "the peace of God." "As I lie sleepless, I think of the eternal insomnia of God." And when her attendant utters a shocked protest, she goes on: "I only quote the Bible. God neither slumbers nor sleeps. Ah, it is the pain of God, not His peace, that passeth understanding."

The cross reared by Caiaphas and Pontius Pilate at the place of a skull is the vivid disclosure of the agony through which the children of men have caused their Father to pass age after age. And Christ who takes on His conscience the sin of his brethren and offers Himself on their behalf is the revelation of the Lord of this and all worlds, who holds Himself responsible for His creatures, who suffers in their pain, who feels implicated in every iniquity of His children, and spends and is spent for their salvation. The cross of wood on which Jesus is nailed is the symbol of an eternal cross in God's heart and conscience. If God be not only transcendent, the Most High, but also immanent, the Most Near, He cannot but suffer as the Companion

[113]

of the unlovely and unloving thoughts and impulses of His sons and daughters. Every neglect and cruelty which they endure at one another's hands is felt as shame by Him, their Divine Kinsman. The sun which shines on evil as well as on good, the rains which fall no less on the unjust than on the just, all the gracious gifts of His providence to the undeserving, all the discipline of the far country for prodigals and every wistful thought of home which rises within them, are a Father's love. In every human voice that pleads with them, in every heart that cares for them, in every life that serves them, His Holy Spirit strives to redeem them. This is the God who is "long beforehand" with our souls and seeks us ere we turn to Him.

If one asks: "Was not Jesus' sacrifice of Himself offered to God?" The answer assuredly is "Yes." "Thy will be done." It was an acceptance of the Father's cup, an acquiescence in His purpose. But it was not a sacrifice to alter God's disposition towards His children. The whole faith of Jesus is utterly opposed to any such conception. Nor does St. Paul, whose theology is sometimes pictured as a misrepresentation of the mind of his Master at this point, depart from it. "God was in Christ reconciling the world unto Himself"; "God commendeth His own love towards us, in that, while we were yet sinners, Christ died for us." Jesus offered a sacrifice to an already Self-sacrificing Father; He made a companion sacrifice through which God's will might be achieved. There is a Divine comradeship in self-giving in Gethsemane and at Calvary. Father and Son are one in conscience, and one in their patient endurance of that which men inflict upon them. God Himself acknowledges this mysterious principle that only by bearing sin can it be destroyed, and that love alone is power where the lives of His children are concerned. Love must suffer where there is sin, and in suffering it redeems. It was a man who knew Calvary who wrote: "God is love."

It may be objected that to say that God, too, submits Himself to this stern necessity of suffering with and for His children in order to save them does not explain His relation to the cross of Christ. If He is Lord of the universe, why has He so constituted it that only by the vicarious suffering of the just for the unjust is life quickened in the spiritually dead? Inasmuch as God is responsible for the structure of the cosmos, why did He make so appalling a tragedy necessary for the Best of men? Bishop Butler was never tired of saying that "the constitution of the world and God's natural government of it, is all mystery." Why anything in earth or sky is as it is, we can never say. John Donne put it:

Why grass is green, or why our blood is red
Are mysteries which none can reach unto.

We have no answers to the riddles of evil and pain, nor can we say why it was necessary that Jesus should suffer and die, and that His followers must share His travail to bring redemption.

Some minds revolt at the belief that a good God can be responsible for a world like ours. When Sir Leslie Stephens died, a writer in *The Bookman* said of him:

He was a rebel against pain, not on his own account, for he stood his trials well, but in a Promethean, man-loving spirit. The sight of the world's tragedy made him an agnostic.

But his fellow-agnostic, Huxley, facing the same painful aspect of life, said:

I cannot but think that he, who finds a certain proportion of pain and evil inseparably woven up in the life of the very worms, will bear his own strain with more courage and submission; and will, at any rate, view with suspicion those weakly amiable theories of the Divine government, which would have us believe pain to be an oversight and a mistake to be corrected by and by.

Christian believers look out upon a world which is dark with inscrutable puzzles and appalling with cruel suffering; and they turn their eyes to Golgotha, not as to one more instance of irrational, unmerited anguish. Here for them is light. Not light which clears up the reasons for pain and injustice, but light which discloses God Himself suffering in love, and by such suffering bringing life to His children. The cross of Christ is surrounded with mystery; it transcends our interpretations; but it is itself our principal clue to these mysteries. Its results, age after age, are so glorious, that it vindicates both the wisdom and the goodness of God.

Such a God freely forgives. Certain widely used hymns still perpetuate the theory that God pardons sinners because Christ purchased that pardon by His obedience and suffering. But a forgiveness which is paid for is not forgiveness. The God of the prophets and psalmists, the God and Father of Jesus' own teaching, forgives graciously all who turn to Him in penitence. His goodness leads to repentance, and repentance is at once followed by complete restoration to fellowship. The cross is the supreme assurance of His forgiveness, the supreme constraint to repentance, the supreme disclosure of the cost to God of our redemption. Men whose consciences trouble them look at Christ crucified, as the Gospel presents Him, and are convinced that God loves them, that He freely pardons them, and that He gives Himself unstintedly to renew them with His life.

Forgiveness is a word which needs redefining in our Christian speech. It is not a calling bygones bygones. There can be no bygones in human character. Our past remains part of us. There is no device by which a man can annul anything which he has thought or felt or done, no means by which he can cleave his heart in twain, as Hamlet bids his mother, and throw the worser part of it away, and live the purer with the other half. There is no cleansing blood which can wipe out the record of what has been. The past is built into the fabric of our spirits. Our current psychology insists on that. In each of us there is a racial past, developed under other conditions, which has to be disciplined to fit it for life in Christian society; and in each one of us there is his own past—the inhibitions and complexes and twists and biases, as well as the results of good influences and training, which have accumulated in him from prenatal days. This is "the deep that coucheth beneath" the surface of every man's conscious life. In it are what theology has called original sin and actual transgressions.

And just because our past remains with us it can be repaired. It has not slipped through our fingers, like flowing water; it is not beyond our reach; it is part of our nature to be moulded and manipulated and, by God's grace, turned to good account, however disgracefully we have come by it. God's forgiveness does not put it away. He lays hold on it with us, and refashions it. Whatever injuries we may have caused others, we must do our utmost to make good. What is forgiven is not our doings or misdoings, but ourselves. The instant we turn in penitence, we are at once received.

That was the Gospel before Calvary; it is the Gospel of which Calvary makes us even more certain. The past continues. Saul the persecutor is still part of Paul the apostle of Christ, now transformed in him into an impetus to passionate service of the Master for whose sake his victims had suffered. Myers makes Paul pray: "Purge from the sin, but never from the pain." The cross does not cancel sins; it does something far better. It transfigures the sin-distorted character so that the remembrance of the sins and their very consequences become factors in the new life.

If we had the story of the prodigal twenty years later, we should not find that his body ceased to show the results of his life with harlots. The effects of that life must be carried till death. Nor would the memory of the pain he had caused his father, nor of the social harm which he had done in lowering the morals of the community be effaced. All his past would remain; but in his father's company it would be transformed into added incentives to fulfil his father's wishes and make the community proof against temptations to spendthrift living and harlotry.

The cross of Christ is not a means of procuring forgiveness: the Father waits to be gracious. It is the symbol of an Elder Brother who went into the far country to manifest the Father's forgiving love; who risked death at the hands of strangers to the Father's heart, that prodigals might know it, and be drawn home. This is what forgiveness costs; none dare receive it as a cheap gift. God could not make us know and feel His love without this awful sacrifice; we cannot accept it without contrite hearts.

Above all Christ crucified is the most compelling evidence that a forgiving and redeeming God lives and rules in this world. A few years ago when that devout Christian mystic, Baron von Hügel, died, Mr. Claude Montefiore concluded a review of his contributions to religious knowledge in *The Jewish Guardian* thus:

The books, great as they may be, are but a fraction of the man. The great scholar-saint was much more than any book, and a much greater evidence than any written words of the God in whom he so passionately believed. In spite of all the appalling perplexities of evil, I find it harder still to think of von Hügel as a toss-up. Somehow for such souls as his, one seems to need a God to account for them.

How much more when one thinks of Christ crucified—thinks of Him in the light of all that His life and death have wrought through the centuries for the transformation and ennoblement of millions of every race, does it seem impossible to think of Him as a toss-up? There is at the core of the universe That which is capable of producing Him and of working with Him. And when we ask what That is, no explanation seems to serve but His own—a God of love. He comes from such a God; He accomplishes His will; He makes Him known and felt redeemingly.

And to be redeemed by and to this gracious Father is to follow Christ with His cross as the standard and inspiration of our thought and sympathy and labor, and to be incorporated by Him into a fellowship—the Church which is His Body—whose task is to make men feel it, too, is no toss-up, for its ministry discloses God, the God whom men need and who needs them.

WHAT MUST WE DO BECAUSE OF IT?

CHAPTER IV

S T. PAUL, who spoke of Christ crucified as the wisdom and power of God,
found in the cross the guide and compulsion to a new life. We have looked at its
theology, let us consider its ethic.

In Jesus on the way to Calvary we see One
who is governed by no external law. There
are no rules of right and wrong which direct
Him to this vicarious Self-offering. He is
impelled by an inward Spirit, and is feeling
His way to His Father's will. Life is a series
of adventures prompted by love. He finds
guidance and inspiration in the experiences of
His predecessors; He draws upon the religious heritage for His ideals. But He cannot follow them slavishly. He appraises them
with His own moral judgment; He tests them;
and amid perplexities and mental struggle He
arrives at His own solution of God's purpose
for Him. There are some lines of Walt Whit-

man on the experimental spirit in which a
man must discover his obligations:

A noiseless, patient spider
I mark'd where, on a little promontory it stood
    isolated,
Mark'd how to explore the vacant vast sur-
    rounding,
It launch'd forth filament, filament, filament
    out of itself,
Ever unreeling them, ever tirelessly speeding
    them.

And you, O my soul, where you stand,
Surrounded, detached, in measureless oceans
    of space,
Ceaselessly musing, venturing, throwing,
    seeking the spheres to connect them;
Till the bridge you will need is form'd—till
    the ductile anchor hold,
Till the gossamer thread you fling catch
    somewhere, O my soul.

If our interpretation of our Lord's mind be
not altogether incorrect, it was by a similar
tentative advance of His conscience that at
length He found sure footing in His Father's
will for Him.

The life of a follower of Jesus is not and cannot be a life under law. Jesus never gave an ethical code, nor did He find in the Scriptures of His people such a code. One should not quote His sayings as binding law upon a moral question like divorce and remarriage, nor cite His example as decisive authority on a citizen's duty in respect of national defense. Had He been a Guide of this sort to contemporaries in first-century Palestine, He could not have been the Leader of mankind generation after generation under circumstances unlike those of His time. He gave the world His Spirit—the Spirit of faith and love which took Him to Golgotha. That Spirit prompts His disciples to similar moral adventures in their day. This is not to disregard His teaching or make light of His example; it is from them that we obtain and constantly renew our supply of His Spirit. But He has set no rigid pattern to be copied; that would destroy the ethical initiative which He Himself displayed. There is no "Jesus-stereotype" cramping living Christians in a first-century mold. Nor has He given us ready-made solutions of our personal or social problems. We cannot speak of any political or economic arrangements as the *Christian* social order. Absolutists continually try from His words and life to set forth such an authoritarian standard. It might mean progress beyond present moral attainment, but ultimately it would mean moral stultification. It would set the goal towards which we aspire; but the goal would become a terminus to our advance. His Spirit is to lead us not only in time but eternally. By the light of Christ the Christian continues to feel his way towards his Father's purpose, and that purpose unfolds age after age, and knows no end.

The preacher has much to do in creating in His people a willingness to undertake ethical experiments. Christianity has so commonly been conceived as a fixed law, and so rarely as a moral venture. The cross seems to be the point at which this can be made most plain. Jesus had no precedent for going to Calvary. There were times when He Himself was uncertain of His course. But as He lived loyally and daringly, He was led, and

led surely. That is the spirit in which respon-
sibilities must be faced and problems thought
through. We are not to uphold existing
standards of goodness; we are to create with
Christ a new earth. It is this creative force
which is the power of God, and it is to be discovered in Christ crucified.

Some may feel that this attitude of moral
experimentation casts aside the authority of
Jesus. His interest, however, was not in getting men to *obey* Him but to *follow* Him.
He did not desire replicas of Himself but
comrades in His pioneering enterprise. His
abiding authority consists in His power to
render His followers discontented with anything in themselves or in their world at vari-
ance with Him, to enlist them to fight with
Him to amend it, and to reinforce them in
their struggle so that they come off "more
than conquerors." And this sovereignty He
exercises supremely from the cross. "He
reigns from the tree."

This insistence on venturesomeness gives
us the angle from which to interpret such
sayings of Jesus as "If any man would be My

disciple, let him take up his cross and follow Me," and "He that would save his life shall lose it." They are not appeals to asceticism, although they involve rigorous self-discipline. Much less are they appeals to patient submission to repressive circumstances. They are challenges to the hazards of a bold ethical enterprise. Human life was cheap in the Roman Empire. Jesus and His listeners had often seen men on the way to their execution. Rome dealt sternly with unruly provincials. Jesus was warning would-be followers of the risks involved. The Kingdom of God as He conceived it was an ethical innovation. A man who became its devotee must expect to "live dangerously" (to borrow Nietzsche's phrase). Jesus knew Himself a moral pioneer. His followers must share with Him the precarious conditions of the frontier. And throughout the New Testament the cross is the conspicuous mark of this moral frontier. Repeatedly Christians are reminded that we must go as far as that in forgiveness, in patience, in love. St. Paul's letters abound in commands to stop nowhere short of the cross in our endurance and service of men. "Even as Christ," or "as God in Christ," so are Christians to bear and to love. A significant saying comes to us from a Christian of the second century: "Our boundary-line is the cross of Christ."

A serious difficulty with the Christian Church age after age is that its members limit their liabilities as followers of Christ. They are prepared to go certain lengths in loyalty to Him, but they are unwilling to go farther. They will be His disciples in Galilee, but they are not ready with Him to set their faces towards Jerusalem. An eminent Roman Catholic teacher of the last generation, Père Gratry, accuses Protestants of removing the cross not only from their churches, but from their lives:

Protestantism is, in its essence, the abolition of sacrifice. To abolish mortification, abstinence and fasting; to abolish the necessity of good works, effort, struggle, virtue; to shut up sacrifice in Jesus alone and not let it pass to us; no more to say, as St. Paul did, I fill up that which is wanting in the sufferings of Christ, but rather to say to Jesus on His cross—Suffer alone, O Lord—there is Protestantism.

We resent such a misrepresentation; but unquestionably the Protestant nations have been the leading exponents of the comfortable life. Many have pointed out the close connection between Calvinism and Capitalism. The release of man's spirit wrought by the Reformation, and the impulse given him by the great Genevan leader to master the earth and subdue its resources to God's kingdom and human well-being, have set Protestant Christians in the forefront of those who control the world's resources. Suffering and want seem to us enemies of the race to be slain. And in a sense they are. We cannot believe that He who gives us all things richly to enjoy is pleased with "mortification, abstinence and fasting," nor do we see anything but a return to a lower ethical level in commending these or any other good works as meritorious. But that is not to say that in following Christ we dare stop short of the painful. We do not make painfulness a test

[134]

of virtue, but we must seriously question a loyalty to Jesus which does not carry a follower the length of sacrifice. In our preaching we must keep insisting that the cross is the limit to which we are prepared to advance in forgiveness, in toleration, in service. To refuse to go so far, is to part company with Christ.

There can be no question but that Church membership has been made too cheap. It has become largely a convention. At a certain age all young people are expected to be received into the communion of the Church in which they have been reared. Seldom is the hardness of the life with Jesus frankly set before them. Nor do the mass of the members of the Christian Church give the impression of having embarked upon a hazardous and straining enterprise. They are living in a thoroughly settled region remote from the moral frontier. They are following precedents, and moving in beaten paths, not exploring new districts of justice, kindness and faithfulness. They do not expect to be exposed to danger. This renders Church membership a tame affair in the eyes of many, and robs it of what originally was its strongest appeal. Followers of Jesus are in every generation a company of revolutionists who turn their world upside down wherever they do not find it love-side up. Revolutions are always perilous for those who engage in them. At present our churches draw and hold the settled and cramp or repel the venturesome, which is precisely the reverse of the New Testament Church. The appeal to enter the fellowship of the Church should be a summons to risk everything for Christ's sake. In 1830 Benjamin Constant, the French philosopher, received a message from his friends in Paris who were overthrowing the Bourbons: "A terrible game is being played here; our heads are in danger; come and add yours." He came. That was the appeal of Jesus to His followers, a call which won home with added realism after Golgotha.

And when the hazard of suffering is accepted, the cross throws further light on the way in which a son of God must endure. Jesus does not view pain as desirable. There is no hint in His teaching that one should seek it for its sanctifying effect. He is at a far remove from the longing for martyrdom of an Ignatius of Antioch. But when suffering has to be faced, He refuses the proffered opiate which would dull His sense. He will "taste the whole of it," remain master of Himself throughout the ordeal and use it for His Father's purpose.

Sir Leslie Stephen once wrote that "great art is produced by taking an exceptionally delicate nature and mangling it slowly under the grinding wheels of the world." It is a much too passive description of the great artist. The mangling of the wheels of the world may be beyond his power to avert, but he must so control himself under them and so use their mangling that it helps him achieve his end. It is what one does with one's suffering which counts. A patient dying of cancer said: "I wish that I could gather up into my own pain all that the world must suffer from cancer and pay the whole debt as I go." That is the utterance of a heroic spirit wistful of being offered vicariously. It was thus

that Jesus acquiesced in and employed the
awful ordeal of His scourging and crucifixion.

In our own day this has been interpreted
for us by a brilliant young English writer,
Katherine Mansfield, stricken with tubercu-
losis and entering in her Journal: "Life is—
getting a new breath. Nothing else counts."
But she has learned how pain is to be met and
employed. Here is what she calls her "confession":

There is no limit to human suffering.
When one thinks: "Now I have touched the
bottom of the sea—now I can go no deeper,"
one goes deeper. I thought last year in Italy,
Any shadow more would be death. But this
year has been so much more terrible.

I do not want to die without leaving a record of my belief that suffering can be overcome. For I do believe it. What must one
do? There is no question of what is called
"passing beyond it." This is false.

One must submit. Take it. Be overwhelmed.
Accept it fully. Make it *part of life*.

Everything in life that we really accept un-
dergoes a change. So suffering must become

[138]

Love. . . . I must put my agony into something, change it.

It is to lose oneself more utterly, to love more deeply, to feel oneself part of life—not separate.

And she ends with a prayer:

O Life! accept me—make me worthy—teach me.

Even as she writes, her soul is wrung, and she adds pathetically:

It is hard—it is hard to make a good death.

The cross of Christ leaves suffering still a mystery, but He shows us clearly what to do with it, and this young English novelist had caught His meaning with singular insight.

The suffering of which we have been speaking has been physical pain; and with the experience of Jesus before us it is clear that His suffering was not mainly physical. He was undergoing the cross mentally long before the nails were driven through His hands and feet. Bernard Shaw has said: "You must

[139]

either share the guilt of the world, or go to another planet." That is unquestionable; but how does a man react to the guilt in which he feels himself involved? Does he accept it as the unavoidable result of human ignorance? Or is the world's condition intolerable to his conscience? After the passage of the Fugitive Slave Law, Emerson in an address at Concord said:

There is infamy in the air. I have a new experience. I wake in the morning with a painful sensation which I carry about all day, and which, when traced home, is the odious remembrance of that ignominy, which robs the landscape of beauty, and takes the sunshine out of every hour.

There is something akin to that in the experience of Jesus. He was struggling with some such dark mystery when He was driven of the Spirit from the Jordan, where He had stood among the penitent throngs at the Baptism, to the lonely conflict with the powers of evil in the wilderness. Before that, in the quiet of Nazareth, it may have been the painful effect upon His mind and heart of the village life in Galilee and the state of Church and nation, which prepared Him for John's message of repentance and which gave Him eyes for the meaning of the portrayal of the Servant of the Lord in the second part of Isaiah.

The Bible has many instances of the value of a conscientious minority. The young priest Phinehas at Shittim, outraged at an act of immoral disloyalty to Jehovah, is jealous with God's jealousy, and makes atonement for the people. Abraham is assured that were there ten righteous men in Sodom, the city would be spared. Jeremiah hunts for even one conscientious inhabitant in Jerusalem, confident that his presence in it will save the city. And Ezekiel sees in vision the heavenly inquisitors going through Jerusalem to place a Divine mark on the foreheads of the men "that sigh and cry over all the abominations that are done in the midst thereof." Where there is a remnant, however small, who care intensely for the quality of the community's life, and who suffer at its apostasy from the Divine ideal, there is hope. A very little conscience, like dynamite, can produce such vast results, if only it becomes explosive.

It is our duty as preachers to cultivate in ourselves and our hearers sensitive consciences. There are many factors which detach us from our fellow-mortals. So praiseworthy a quality as a sense of humor makes us stand off while we smile at the pettinesses of men. Jesus could both smile, as the playfulness of some of His metaphors witness, and feel intensely. He could speak ironically of the Pharisees, straining out the gnat while they gulped down the camel, and in the same breath disclose an aching heart: "O Jerusalem, Jerusalem." Indeed one does not know whether the tone in which He uttered His "Woe unto you" may not have made it "Alas for you!" Miss Thackeray described humor as "thinking in fun while we feel in earnest." It was that which Jesus possessed. Our task is to bring home to our people by every device available their solidarity with those whom they criticize, those at whom they laugh, those upon whom they look down. We

are not going to get forward in race relations, in international good will, in industrial
peace, until we acquire the capacity to suffer
in the follies and failures and misfortunes of
others. We find denunciation so much easier
than compassion; and the cross on Calvary
had its origin in a compassionate heart.

Ministers of Christ's gospel, above all
others, must have this vicarious conscience.
One is shocked to meet a minister who speaks
disparagingly of his people, or who scolds
them from the pulpit, or who blames them for
their faults or their worldliness. He has not
entered into His Lord's mind even at its first
disclosure at the Jordan, let alone in its unveiling at Calvary. If our people are not what
they should be, who is more chargeable than
we, their leaders in the life with God? Their
failure to be ruled by the Spirit of Christ may
well be traceable in part to some kindred failure in ourselves. You recall Christina Ros-
setti's denunciation of another:

Clearly his own fault. Yet, I think,
My fault in part, who did not pray
But lagged and would not lead the way.

[143]

It is only from ambassadors of Christ, who share His sense of guilt for the sins of those to whom they preach, that the message of reconciliation will be heard with moving power. Sin-bearing ministers alone can represent the Saviour of sinners.

And more even than the preacher must the pastor possess towards those he would serve this sense of relatedness in their defects. The late Baron von Hügel, a most painstaking and skilful lay shepherd of souls, writing to his niece, a brilliant young woman, in a marvellously frank exchange of letters, tells her how in his feeble health he had been lying awake with her difficulties on his heart and mind. He writes:

I wonder whether you realize a deep, great fact? That souls—all human souls—are deeply interconnected? That (I mean) we cannot only pray for each other, but *suffer* for each other? That these long trying wakings, that I was able to offer them to God and to Christ for my child—that He might ever strengthen, sweeten, steady her in her true, simple, humble love and dependence upon

Him. Nothing is more real than this interconnection—this gracious power put by God
Himself into the very heart of our infirmities.

It is ministers who appreciate and know this
"interconnection" who can in some measure
understand and interpret the vicarious life
and death of Christ.

His biographer, speaking of Woodrow
Wilson as professor at Princeton, dwells on
the pain which his fastidious mind endured
from the slovenly vernacular of the students.
"I positively am not able to read and correct
more than ten or twelve papers a day," he
told a colleague. For the same reason he
dreaded to listen to intercollegiate debates, although he gave himself generously in coach-
ing the Princeton debaters. The same colleague tells us:

I have seen him pacing back and forth
through the ambulatory of the Commencement Hall when a debate was in progress, unable to keep away, and still less able to sustain
the verbal affront which the crudeness and
immaturity of his protégés were almost certain to inflict.

It is an instance of that "double feeling," mentioned in the last chapter—unable to keep away, and less able to endure the pain of listening to inept presentation of argument.

A Christian must be in like revolt against the crudities and carelessness of man's life with man, and against the ignorance and forgetfulness of man's mind towards God, and at the same time in such sympathy with every unloving and unbelieving brother that he cannot hold aloof and dissociate himself from him.

It is our task as ambassadors of Christ to draw men together into one commonwealth of spirit, one household of faith and love. And in the New Testament it is the cross which links men to one another as well as reconciling them to God. It is at Calvary that St. Paul sees the middle wall of partition between Jew and non-Jew broken down. When he faces breaches between fellow-Christians, he sets before the quarrelling or grudge-bearing the cross of Christ: "Walk in love, even as Christ also loved you and gave Himself up for you." The fourth evangelist interprets

Christ as dying "that He might gather together into one the children of God that are scattered abroad."

Those who lived and ministered during the years of the Great War may have shared the experience of the writer, who month after month found haunting his mind the text: "God gave unto us the ministry of reconciliation." Amid the passions and hatreds of that appalling day when by every device imaginable men were butchering one another on a wholesale scale, what could a minister of the Gospel do to discharge this God-committed duty? The text burned itself into his heart and was a daily discomfort and misery to him.

And to-day that ministry of reconciliation is as sorely needed, and happily can be more readily fulfilled. But we fulfil it in the manner of St. Paul only as we preach the constraining love of Christ in the unifying act of His Self-offering for all at Golgotha. There is a good deal of preaching about brotherhood which is very superficial, and consequently futile. We are not seeking to induce men and women to overcome their prejudices and to feel kindly towards mankind. No doubt that would be a decided advance; but it would not take them to Christian brotherhood. Nor are we promoters of good will, after the manner of transoceanic fliers and many excellent internationalists—admirable as good will is. Such better feeling stops far short of fellowship in the love of Christ. We are creators with God of a new conscience and a new heart —the conscience and heart revealed at Golgotha. We dare not satisfy ourselves with doing less, and we shall attempt much less unless we persistently keep taking the divisive factors in human relations direct to Calvary.

Let me illustrate with a few examples: At the close of the Great War an attempt was made by the representatives of the victorious Allies at Paris to force Germany to admit guilt for bringing on the world catastrophe. The result was bitter resentment on the part of the German people, and frequent protests ever since on the part of numerous writers in the Allied countries who have pointed out the responsibility of other nations as well for the conflict. The conscience of mankind has not been satisfied. Had the righteousness of the Allied nations been akin to that of Christ, we should all have penitently placed ourselves beside our foes, searching our ways and acknowledging the motives and practices which had produced suspicion, fear and bitterness, and making confession of our sin which had been visited by such appalling judgment. There is no question but that the conscience of Germany would have responded. We were all guilty, if in varying degrees, and in the effusion of blood and tears we suffered with and for each other. Had we so interpreted our common experience, and had we together repented of those sins of greed and pride and reliance on brute force which led us to mutual slaughter, the out-poured blood of millions would have proved redemptive, and these post-war years would have told a very different story. A commonwealth of nations might have been born, with assurance of vigorous and happy growth, out of such birth-throes of penitent sorrow. We did not know how to bear one another's sins and to find fellowship in common repentance and

confession. True brotherhood is not easily
come by. The nations labored, but had not
moral strength to bring forth.

In the industrial realm we cannot look for
comradeship so long as our economic strife is
treated as the inevitable clash of *haves* versus
have-nots, and various devices and compro-
mises assayed to foster good feeling. This is
to heal lightly a deep-seated moral malady.
We need to take our economic ills to the cross
—to bring home to consciences what men,
women and little children suffer in casual em-
ployment, in work into which they cannot put
themselves, in hours of labor which break up
family life and render education and wholesome recreation impossible, in conditions
which stultify the mind and numb the soul of
workers as well as wearing out the body, in
relations which breed servility and envy and
ill-will and poison the heart. Nor is the conscience which needs stimulation all on one
side. There is social guilt in all work which
is not viewed as ministry, in all gain which is
not recognized as compensation for service,
in all wealth which is not held and used with

[150]

scrupulous honor as a trust for the community. Among those reputed successful there are tragic moral disasters for which we cannot evade responsibility. The hardening which our competitive system produces, the self-seeking it encourages, the shrewdness it applauds, the power it confers on possessors of large means which renders them arbitrary and dictatorial—these are results in which we are all involved. And when some over-reaching and rascally Dives is exposed in a scandal, it will not do for us to execrate him and make him a scape-goat to be laden with our collective acquisitiveness. On those rare occasions when such an one is pilloried, the community ought to place itself beside him in public shame. We have all aided in producing him. He epitomizes what we know exists in us all. His punishment may be salutary in putting the fear of consequences upon similarly tempted men; but it ought to have redemptive effects on society, and this can be only as we acknowledge ourselves implicated in his criminality and really suffer in his disgrace.

Above all, it is in our treatment of the wrong-doer that we need to be reminded of the cross. We are grateful for the light our psychiatrists are throwing on the motives and causes of crime. We are thankful for the gains in the educational handling of sinners against society, which so often transforms them, or at any rate does not as surely damn them as did the clumsier methods of the past. But there remains an appalling problem in the huge prison population in all civilized lands and in the large numbers outside prison walls afflicted with the same anti-social tendencies. When we send a fellow-mortal, however depraved, to the electric chair, we cannot feel that we deal with him in the manner of God at Golgotha. No doubt there is much suffering of the innocent with and for the guilty in connection with the administration of our criminal law. One thinks of the families of those in prison, of the social disgrace which they feel, of the agony of soul undergone by mothers and wives sitting in our court-rooms and visiting loved ones in their cells, of the handicaps of poverty and suspicion upon help-

[152]

less children. And this suffering of the innocent sometimes has redemptive consequences.
But in the whole process there is wanting the
voluntary sin-bearing of the Son of God, the
taking and sharing of the guilt of the sinner
by those who love.

It is not easy to be concrete. Most of us
have known instances, however, when really
Christlike souls have come forward and sac-
rificed themselves. A young man's defalca-
tion was assumed by an elderly kinswoman
who gave up the fortune with which she had
been provided by her dead husband, and she
looked forward to an old age without comforts and dependent upon the pittance she
might earn or the young man be able and
sufficiently honorable to supply. And such instances have made more real and cogent for
us the sacrifice at Calvary. But we wait for
more imagination and more skill, as well as
for finer consciences, to remould our penal
system and to fill our communities with more
redemptive forces to bring sinners against
society to feel the transforming love of God.
Until we manage to do this, we cannot look

for their reconciliation to the community and their restoration to fellowship. As ambassadors of Christ we cannot be content to preach and try to exemplify less than this.

Again we need to stress the social effect of the goodness of individuals who themselves represent and embody the ethical ideal. We have talked, perhaps, too much of vicarious suffering and too little of vicarious righteousness. Of that Jeremiah and Ezekiel were thinking, and the historian who records God's willingness to spare Sodom could ten righteous men be found in the city. Moral pioneers alter the spiritual horizon. Jesus, by setting the standard of love beyond the hitherto accepted boundaries, altered the map of obligation for mankind. He brought heights within our ken which were not there before, and which tempt us to scale them. We live in a different world ethically because Jesus has lived and died.

There is a striking illustration of the effect of a singularly elevated life from the realm of literature. In 1900, when the health of Tolstoy was reported to be failing, Anton Tchekov wrote to a literary friend:

WHAT MUST WE DO BECAUSE OF IT?

I am afraid of Tolstoy's death. If he were to die there would be a big vacuum in my life. Firstly, I never loved anyone as I loved him; I am not a believing man, but of all beliefs I consider his faith the nearest and most akin to me. Secondly, while Tolstoy is in literature, it is easy and pleasant to be a writer; even to be aware that one has done nothing and is doing nothing is not so terrible, since Tolstoy does enough for all. His work serves as a justification of all the hopes and anticipations built upon literature. Thirdly, Tolstoy stands firmly, his authority is immense, and while he lives, bad tastes in literature, banality of every kind, impudent or lachrymose, all the bristling exasperated vanities will remain far away, deep in the shade. His moral authority alone is capable of maintaining on a certain height the so-called literary moods and currents.

One scarcely needs to draw the analogy. Only our Lord's moral authority was not limited to His lifetime. His death vastly enhanced it. Men who have difficulty in believing, look wistfully to the faith of One who could live such a life and die such a death. With Christ towering above us, we feel the nobility of trying to be servants of God and man, and even when we do little, rejoice that He has done enough for all. Or rather, we take our poor best and view it in the light of His cross, and are confident that whatever likeness it has to that goodness will give it something of Christ's own abiding power.

And this brings us finally to the basis of a life of venturesome love, such as that to which the Crucified summons His followers. Is it a desperate effort to live for and die for a purpose which may be defeated, because the whole scheme of things is indifferent to our attempt? Or is it a venture which the universe itself helps on, because at its centre there is a Conscience akin to that of the vicarious Giver of His life at Calvary? Is not this the ultimate religious problem which every ethical thinker must face?

There is much social passion to-day, which bears the marks of the Lord Jesus in its consecration, but which is devoid of His underlying faith. Thomas Hardy puts on the lips of a vanishing God lines which he entitles "A Plaint to Man."*

(*By permission of The Macmillan Company, publishers.)

WHAT MUST WE DO BECAUSE OF IT?

When you slowly emerged from the den of
    time,
And gained percipience as you grew,
And fleshed you fair out of shapeless slime,

Wherefore, O man, did there come to you
The unhappy need of creating Me—
A Form like your own—for praying to?

'Such a forced device,' you may say, 'is meet
For easing a loaded heart at whiles;
Man needs to conceive of a mercy-seat.

Somewhere above the gloomy aisles
Of this wailful world, or he could not bear
The irk no local hope beguiles.'

But since I was framed in your first de-
    spair
The doing without Me has had no play
In the minds of men whom shadows scare.

And now that I dwindle day by day
Beneath the deicide eyes of seers
In a light that will not let me stay,

And to-morrow the whole of Me disappears,
The truth should be told, and the fact be faced
That had best been faced in earlier years:

The fact of life with dependence placed
On the human heart's resource alone,
In brotherhood bonded close and graced

With loving kindness fully blown,
And visioned help unsought, unknown.

But the resources of human hearts are so
pathetically meagre and can do so pitiably little against the storms of the cosmic weather.
Brotherhood may aid vastly in rendering human existence tolerable and happy, but of
what avail is it against a universe, if the universe be indifferent or hostile to love? Men
will do much for brotherhood, they will lay
down their lives for love provided they believe that they are not sacrificing themselves
in a forlorn hope. Can we preach the cross
hopefully? Is it possible to produce "lovingkindness fully blown" where visioned help is
unknown? The lovingkindness of Jesus at
Golgotha, than which none has been so completely blossoming and fruitful, was grown in
a very different climate.

We cannot preach the cross and expect to
create a commonwealth of similar devotees of

[158]

man unless we also preach the resurrection. And unhappily much of our Easter preaching seems to disregard the connection between the cross and the return in triumph to His disciples. Many an Easter sermon is a proclamation of the Christian hope of another life beyond the grave. This may be entirely appropriate, but let us remember that resurrection is not identical with immortality. Very few, if any, of those who crucified Jesus thought that they were ending His existence altogether. Some Sadducees and possibly some Romans may have thought so; but the overwhelming majority of His opponents supposed that His spirit would continue to live on somewhere. They did not wish Him alive in Jerusalem or in Galilee, where in their eyes He was a menace to the Jewish Church and a disturbing factor in the Roman Empire. They were resolved to rid their world of Him: that He would exist in some other world did not concern them. Nor did Jesus Himself, as He went to Calvary, pray for immortality. He was not thinking of His own survival. He had "lost Himself" (to use His own phrase). All that He longed for was to see God's kingdom come and His will done here on the earth and among the children of men. The Easter faith in which the Christian Church was born is not that Jesus survived death and gave evidence of such survival, as for example spiritualists fancy they receive communications from the dead assuring them of their continuing existence; but that Jesus was alive in power with and among His disciples in this world, whence His foes had banished Him, and was going on with His work in and through His Church.

We need to stress the difference between the publicity of the crucifixion before priests and scribes and soldiers and multitudes and the privacy of the appearances to individuals, like Peter and James, Mary Magdalene and Saul of Tarsus, or to small groups of friends, like the two at Emmaus, or the ten or eleven in the Upper Room, or the seven by Gennesaret, or even to the five hundred brethren. These, with the possible exception of Saul, were already believers in Christ. Some spiritual preparation and capacity is essential to perception of the risen Lord. The resurrection is not an event in the physical world, as we ordinarily understand it. There is no appearance to the soldiers, or to the Sanhedrin, or to Pontius Pilate, or to the crowds in the bazars of Jerusalem. But Jesus is alive with and in His own. His life is like His Father's of which He says, "My Father who is in secret." And as such Jesus is a mightier force in Judæa and Galilee and the Roman world *post mortem* than *ante mortem*. That is undeniable, and that is the main point when we are thinking of the connection between the Life laid down in love and the character of the universe.

For what is at stake in the brutal death of Jesus is the kind of world in which we live. Is it soulless? Does it care nothing at all what man does or does not do? Or is it responsive to such love as Christ's on the cross? If Jesus can be permanently beaten, His purpose frustrated, His hopes brought to naught, then in what an appalling universe we find ourselves! Would Jesus wish to go on living in it, doomed to labor and suffer forever in vain? Could His friends wish for Him an existence in which again and again His pioneering conscience will bring Him to a Gethsemane and a Golgotha without result? That would make the universe a series of torture-chambers for spirits akin to His, a chain of hells for the loving.

He cherished no illusions about the cosmic weather. He foresaw upon every man's life and work rains descending, floods coming and winds blowing. But He believed that it was possible to dig deep and base a foundation on rock. And Easter, however you explain the precise mode in which He resumed His intercourse with His followers, is the vindication of His faith. "Then the foundations of the world were laid bare." It is not soulless. The moral venture of Calvary was not futile. Such love is shown to have allies in the very fabric of things. Jesus could not be holden of death. He remains our most vital and potent Contemporary these centuries after His enemies believed Him dead and buried. A living God responded to the trust reposed in Him by this Son, and brought Him, and is

still bringing Him, to victory. We hold up
Christ crucified as the ethical ideal with confidence. This is the motive which works,
which conquers, which more than conquers.
To follow Christ, sharing the fellowship of
His sufferings, is to know the power of His
resurrection.

And obviously in such a universe a personality like Christ's, yes the personalities of the
least of His brethren, have abiding signifi-
cance. Such a God as the Easter triumph
demonstrates will not scrap a spirit after He
has used Him in His service. He means too
much to His brethren and to His Father.

And the further life to which we look forward in the light of the resurrection of Jesus
is a life which we can interpret only by the
cross. It is an existence, as we forefancy it,
in which such moral pioneering goes on, where
the dominant motive is the love we know at
Calvary. It is a life where the loving, and
the loving only, are at home with the Lord.
A limitless horizon stretches out before us
when we think of the matured spirits of followers of Christ going forward with Him

from glory to glory and from strength to strength. And the radiance which suffuses our Christian hope comes from that black event of long ago where Jesus hung and suffered and died outside the gate of Jerusalem. For in the holy city of our expectation the light thereof is the Lamb.

... strength to
... And the ... when ...
... Christians ... ... that ...
... of love, and where Jesus ...
... and died, which the ... of ...
... in the holy ... of our ...
... light ... to the Land.